Celebrate the Seasons

with

Ribbon Embroidery by Machine

Marie Duncan and Betty Farrell

Copyright © 1998 by Marie Duncan and Betty Farrell
All Rights Reserved
Published by

 **krause publications**
700 East State St., Iola, WI 54990-0001
Telephone (715) 445-2214

Please call or write for our free catalog of publications. Our toll-free number to place an order or obtain a free catalog is (800) 258-0929 or please use our regular business telephone (715) 445-2214 for editorial comment and further information.

Cover design by Jan Wojtech
Book design by Mary Lou Marshall and Jan Wojtech
Photography by Kris Kandler
Illustrations by Marie Duncan
Manufactured in the United States of America

Library of Congress Cataloging-in-Publication Data

Duncan, Marie and Farrell, Betty
Celebrate the seasons with ribbon embroidery by machine

        p. 112

ISBN 0-87341-623-6

1. Ribbon embroidery   2. Embroidery, machine   3. Title

                                           98-84105
                                               CIP

Introduction

Season - sea-son (se-zan)

Noun

1. a. One of the four natural divisions of the year, spring, summer, fall & winter.
   b. The two divisions of the year, rainy and dry.
2. A recurrent period marked by certain occurrences or festivities: the holiday season, the tomato season.

Verb

1. To enhance the flavor of food by adding salt or other flavoring
2. To add zest or interest to (from Latin: satio, act of sowing)

In nature, the spring season is a time of new growth, the end of a long winter, a time of hope. Flowers burst through the earth, sometimes, even through the snow! They grow so fast, we watch in awe. Regardless of the time of our birth, it is the spring of our lives. We are welcomed by our families, cared for, and nurtured. We grow under the watchful eye of Mother Nature. As we grow, so do the spring flowers, the grasses, trees, and vegetables. It is a favorite season of the year for most of us, somewhat of a new beginning. It is the season in which we celebrate Easter, a celebration of hope, and a magical time for children.

Summer is a time of warmth and growth. The seeds we sowed come to fruition. Flowers bloom and trees and bushes put forth new growth and grow to maturity. In the summer of our lives, we grow into adulthood and leave childhood behind. It is a pleasant time of our lives, free from the stresses that come later in our adult lives. Summer is a time of enjoyment, picnics, graduations, long, lazy days filled with warmth and light.

As we enter autumn, the days are shorter and temperatures cooler. Many of us find the cool, clear, crisp days totally invigorating. It is a time to return to school, return to work after summer vacations and trips, and prepare our homes and lives for the winter to come. It is the time of harvest, to reap the benefit of the labors of the long hot summer. Autumn is a serious time in our lives, the time that as adults we raise our families and bring our careers to full fruition. Autumn is a time when the traditional American holidays begin with Labor Day, followed by Halloween and ending with Thanksgiving.

Winter unofficially starts with the "Christmas Season." As Thanksgiving ends, "the holidays" begin. We celebrate in many different ways. Some are very religious, whether Christian, Jewish, or other, many are elaborate and many are simple. Most fall somewhere between. It is a season to be with family and friends and form new traditions, as well as cherish the old ones as we have through the years. In nature, winter is a time of hibernation, where the animals hole up to be warm and survive the long cold time of the year. Others go south in perpetual pursuit of summer and the resulting warmth. Trees lose their leaves and "wait" out the cold winter. Flowers lie dormant under the frozen earth awaiting the coming of spring. The winter season of our lives is usually one of contentment, sitting back, enjoying the fruits of a lifetime of labor, retirement, grandchildren, and hopefully an easier lifestyle.

Wreath - (reth)

Noun

Pl. wreaths (re-thz, reths)
1. A ring or circular band, as of flowers or leaves
2. A curling or circular form: a wreath of smoke
From Old English - Writha, band

The Greeks bestowed wreaths of leaves or flowers on the winners of sports and poetry contests and on citizens for outstanding public service. Such wreaths or crowns were also worn at weddings and funerals. These traditions were continued by the Romans who awarded wreaths to soldiers who saved the lives of Roman citizens in battle. The most highly prized was the wreath bestowed by a beleaguered garrison or army on the general who rescued them.

We chose the grapevine wreath as the ongoing theme of *Celebrate the Seasons with Ribbon Embroidery by Machine* because the solid base of grapevines endures through the seasons, renewing itself each spring with buds, bearing fruit in summer, to be harvested in fall, and then resting in winter. Even when the grapevines have died, they can be resurrected to be decorated as the wreaths we have portrayed. Decorate the wreath to celebrate the events in your life, the season you are living, and the hopes you have for the future.

This book is dedicated to our grandchildren! Ceilidh Marie was the name given to Marie's grandchild-to-be years before he/she was actually born. She represented a hope for the future and a promise of the wonderful season of life to come, that of a grandmother. "She" turned out to be a "he," Alex, born August 23, 1997! Betty's 12 grandchildren have been a continual source of joy and inspiration. We enjoy watching them in the Spring of their lives now.

Cherish and relish the season you are a part of. We hope you can enjoy ribbon embroidery by machine along with the other techniques offered in *Celebrate the Seasons* as much as we have enjoyed presenting them.

Marie

Betty

Table of Contents

Chapter 1
Supplies

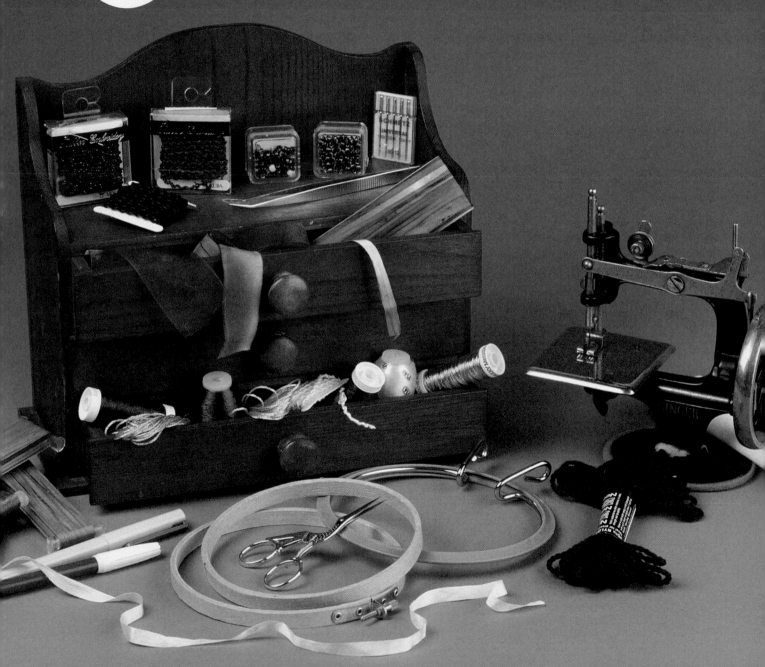

the first few washings. Silk ribbon can be machine dried with no need for pressing. If an item is dry cleaned, caution the dry cleaner not to flatten the design by pressing over it.

We have worked on ready-to-wear garments as well as those we sew ourselves. The secret to success for different fabrics is gearing the type of embroidery to the type of fabric—bolder designs and stitches for heavier fabrics and finer delicate patterns for the lighter weight fabrics.

Hoop

You'll need a 5″-6″ hoop and can choose any type you prefer (wooden, spring, etc.) as long as it fits under the needle of your sewing machine. Be sure it holds the fabric snugly. If you are working on a delicate fabric such as silk or fine cotton, you may want to wrap the hoop with twill tape to reduce the abrasion on the fabric as you place it in the hoop. Knit fabric doesn't require any special attention, but be careful not to stretch it as you place it in the hoop. Spring hoops are better for knits.

In the past few years companies have introduced adhesive stabilizers. Two popular brands are Sulky™ Sticky stabilizer and Filmoplast stic™. If you place this type of stabilizer in a hoop with the sticky side up and lay the fabric on top, you won't need to hoop the fabric. This works great for velvet, terry cloth, or any fabric where the line from the hoop would be noticeable.

Sewing Machine

A sewing machine is essential for creating ribbon embroidery by machine. Any sewing machine will work, since the only stitch you use is the straight stitch. A machine that allows you to lower or cover the feed dogs is an asset and a machine with an electronic needle stop-down setting is a great advantage. The more stitch-by-stitch control you have, the better.

Fabric

Ribbon embroidery is so versatile it can be worked on the finest silk or the heaviest denim or any fabric in between and look great. Silk ribbon can be washed or dry cleaned, so that is not a limitation. We have hand and machine washed embroidered items with good results. Simply follow care instructions for the fabric. On brightly colored silk ribbon it may be prudent to launder the item in cold water for

Thread

Use invisible thread (sometimes called monofilament) in the top and the bobbin. The invisible thread available today is very different from 20 years ago. YLI™, Sulky, Coats & Clark™, and Dritz™ all produce invisible thread in clear or smoke. These are amazingly soft and feel almost like regular thread. Some are nylon and some are polyester. The advantage of using invisible thread is that you don't have to keep changing the thread color. If you are working on very dark ribbons or fabric, you may want to use the smoke color, but clear is translucent so it almost disappears. In most cases the ribbon will cover it anyway.

You can also use polyester or polyester/cotton thread with satisfactory results, but you'll need to change the thread to match the ribbon colors. Polyester and polyester/cotton threads tend to be more visible than invisible thread.

Ribbon

Embroidery ribbon is different from the decorative type of ribbon you buy at a fabric store. It is made of 100% silk or a synthetic such as polyester or rayon and is available at most fabric/sewing stores. Silk embroidery ribbon is extremely soft and pliable. It is this texture that allows you to fold and bend it to form beautiful flowers and foliage! The ribbon comes in 2mm, 4mm, 7mm, and 13mm. The 4mm is the most popular and comes in about 150 colors. The other sizes are available in fewer colors.

Because of the popularity of ribbon embroidery, there are many different brands and types available, including synthetic, rayon, polyester, as well as silk from several different manufacturers. As with anything you buy, some are better quality than others. Be sure the ribbon you choose is colorfast if you intend to wash or dry clean the embroidered item.

Some new ribbons are over-dyed or edge-dyed. In a later chapter we discuss dyeing your own or you can purchase dyed ribbon at most stores that stock silk ribbon. Over-dyed and edge-dyed ribbons give a natural shading appearance when used with solid color ribbons.

There is also a new line of chiffon-type ribbon available. These ribbons are a semi-sheer nylon and are very pliable for machine embroidery. Again, they blend well with regular silk ribbons.

Optional Threads

Occasionally we mention other threads, such as pearl rayon. These are generally heavier weight, crochet-type threads used for detail work. Use these threads like the ribbon, not like thread for the machine. Regular embroidery floss or crochet cotton can be used for these special effects too. Metallic cords, "bumpy" boucles, and fuzzy yarns all have their place, depending on the textures you desire. Mokuba™ offers a nice selection of these different textures, as do "On the Surface" Embellishment Thread assortments which include five yards each of six color-coordinated fibers.

Needles

Always start with a new needle in the sewing machine. Use a size 80/12 Universal needle. If the needle has a burr or rough spot, it will snag the delicate ribbon. Change the needle immediately if snagging occurs.

Markers

Air-soluble markers are available from several suppliers (Collins™, EZ™, Dritz™) in many different colors. An air-soluble marker will evaporate by itself in 12 to 24 hours. There are also fine line markers for intricate work. Chalk pencils or tailor's chalk can be used on dark colors. Just be sure the marks can be removed if they are not completely covered by the embroidery.

Tweezers

Use serger tweezers to hold the ribbon in place as you sew (you may already have some from your serger). We recommend a bent nose tweezer 5″, 6″, or 7″ long. Choose the size most comfortable for you. A trolley needle will also come in handy for holding the ribbon in place.

Chapter 2
Machine Set-Up

R ibbon embroidery can be done on any sewing machine in good running condition. Take a minute to clean out the lint and oil the machine if it normally requires oil. To do ribbon embroidery, set up the machine for free motion work as explained below.

Set-Up

1. Remove the presser foot. If you have snap-on feet, remove the shank that the presser foot attaches to by removing the screw. Consult the owner's manual for details.
2. *Slowly* wind a bobbin with invisible thread—half a bobbin is plenty. Place the bobbin in the machine.
3. Insert a new size 80/12 Universal needle.
4. Raise the presser foot, then thread the machine with invisible thread

5. Drop or cover the feed dogs. (Refer to the directions in the owner's manual for sewing on a button.)
6. If the machine has the option, set the needle stop-down feature to the down position.
7. Note the normal tension setting if it is not marked on the machine. Lower the top tension by about one number.
8. Engage the "slow" speed-setting feature if you have this option.
9. Make a generous sewing area for the hoop by using the flat bed extension to cover the free arm.

Helpful Hints

Follow these guidelines while stitching. Read them before you begin and refer to them if you have a problem.
* Lower the presser foot lever when sewing.
* Raise the presser foot lever when you thread the sewing

machine. (It's harder to notice the presser foot lever without a presser foot attached. Try to get in the habit of lowering the presser foot lever as soon as you put the hoop on your machine.)

* Work with the needle down in the fabric. Set the needle stop-down (if you have that feature on the machine) or stop with it in the down position.

* If you get wads of thread underneath the fabric, the presser foot lever is not down or the thread is not in the tension discs. Rethread the machine and lower the presser foot.

* If the fabric bounces as you sew or the thread breaks frequently, the fabric may not be secured tightly enough in the hoop.

* If the thread breaks too often, put in a new needle or try lowering the tension one more number.

* Don't worry about cutting the ribbon pieces too long. Keep a small container to hold small leftovers from the ends of a design. They will come in handy when you need one petal of a color or to fill in a small space.

* Save your practice projects and use them to make ornaments or crazy patchwork pieces. Only you will know they are scraps.

* Be patient with yourself. Whenever you try a new technique, your production will be slow. Keep at it. With ribbon embroidery, the more you work, the faster and more confident you'll become.

Care of Embroidered Items

Finished ribbon embroidered items need special care. The majority of ribbons we work with can be machine washed and dried *with care*. Turn the garment inside out and set the machine on the gentle cycle. Dry at a low temperature just long enough to dry. Don't use high heat or over-dry. Hand washing and hanging to dry are always safe.

If you're not sure the ribbons you're using are colorfast, pin a test piece to a scrap of white fabric, dip in water, swish, and put in the dryer. If any color runs, it's best to dry clean.

When taking garments to the dry cleaner, ask them to hand press the garments so as to not press over the ribbon embroidery. Pressing will smash it!

When pressing the finished garments yourself, press around the embroidery, not on it. If you need to get between two designs where the iron doesn't fit, try using a sleeve board. Place the embroidery just off the edge and you can get into tight spaces.

Another good way to press finished embroidery is to place it face down on a thick terry towel and gently steam it. The embroidery is pushed down and cushioned by the towel.

A puff iron (smockers love them) is ideal for pressing under ribbon embroidery. You can press the fabric without flattening the ribbon.

If you accidentally press over some embroidery, fluff it with a burst of steam, holding the iron a few inches above the garment.

Free Motion Stitching

If you've done free motion machine embroidery before, you may choose to skip this section. Free motion embroidery looks more difficult than it is. Take the time to practice on a scrap of fabric. Enjoy the freedom this technique offers...once you've mastered the free motion technique you will use it a lot and wonder why it took you so long to try it!

1. Place an 8″ square of fabric in a hoop. If you do hand embroidery, note that here you use the hoop the opposite way. Place the larger ring of the hoop on a flat surface. Lay the fabric on top. Place the smaller ring on top and insert it inside the larger and tighten the screw. Pull the fabric taut. In a spring hoop, it will tighten automatically.

2. Thread the machine and set it up (refer to Machine Set-Up, page 9). When you do free motion stitching, *you* are moving the fabric, the sewing machine is no longer feeding the fabric for you. This enables you to move in any direction—forward, backward, sideways, etc.

3. Place the hoop under the needle with the fabric against the bed of the machine and lower the presser foot. Even though the presser foot has been removed from the machine, you must lower the presser foot lever to engage the tension. If you forget, you'll have wads of thread underneath your work.

4. Take one stitch by manually turning the flywheel towards you one full turn and draw the bobbin thread up so both threads are on top of the fabric. Take three or four stitches in place and snip the thread tails. This is always the way to begin to keep the back neat and tidy. Practice moving the fabric randomly. You can sew sideways, forward, backward, any direction you want. Draw some circles and practice following the lines. Be sure to keep the fabric flat against the bed of the machine. You don't want to lift the hoop. Do this for a few minutes and you should be ready to start ribbon embroidery.

Chapter 3
Stitches

Chain Stitch

The chain stitch is a commonly used embroidery stitch. We use it for roses, stems, initials, outlines, and more. For the basic chain stitch you'll manipulate the ribbon with your hands, so tweezers aren't necessary.

❶ Place the fabric in the hoop with the larger ring on the bottom and place the hoop in the machine. Lower the presser foot lever.

❷ Holding the thread securely, take one stitch and pull the bobbin thread up to the surface. Holding the threads, take a few stitches to anchor the threads and snip off the thread tails.

❸ Take a few stitches in the center of a 10˝- 12˝ length of ribbon.

❹ Hold the ribbon out of the way so it's not caught in the stitching. Stitch forward 1/4˝ on the fabric.

❺ Cross the ribbon in front of the needle.

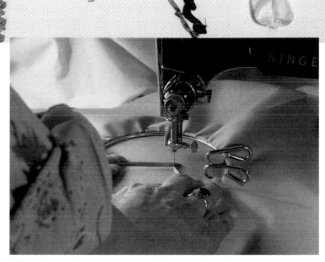

When beginning the chain stitch, start by stitching in the center of the ribbon.

Adjust the tension on the ribbon so it's not too tight or loose. A soft fullness is desirable. Stitch across the crossed ribbon, being sure to sew a stitch or two in the ribbon itself.

❻ Keeping the ribbon out of the way, stitch 1/4˝. Again cross the ribbon in front of the needle and stitch across it. Repeat these steps— stitch, cross the ribbon, stitch, cross the ribbon, and so on.

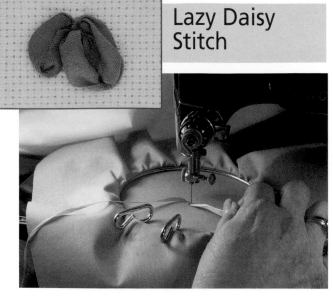

Lazy Daisy Stitch

If you want a squished end, hold the ribbon perpendicular to the needle.

When beginning any stitch except the chain stitch, start by stitching at the end of the ribbon.

The lazy daisy stitch is one of the most commonly used traditional embroidery stitches. We use it for leaves, flowers, foliage, flower centers, and much more. As with all stitches, the width of ribbon you use will determine the finished size of the lazy daisy. Make some with 2mm, 4mm, and 7mm.

1 To sew a lazy daisy stitch, use tweezers to hold the ribbon in place as you sew. Anchor the end of a 12″ length of ribbon by taking a few stitches on it, then hold the ribbon out of the way and stitch out about 1/4″, stopping with the needle down.

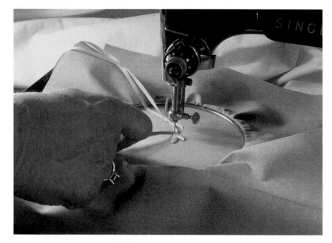

When doing stitches like the lazy daisy, hold the ribbon in place with serger tweezers.

2 Bring the ribbon around the needle and stitch a couple stitches to anchor it. Don't pull it too tight, let it lie comfortably (not too tight, not too loose). The ribbon should lie flat in the center and a bit squished at the ends.

3 Hold the ribbon out of the way and stitch back to the starting point.

4 Bring the ribbon back to the starting point and stitch to anchor it. You don't want it too tight or too loose. Try to shape it a bit, holding it with the tweezers as you sew.

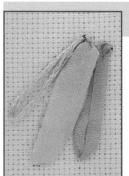

Flat Lazy Daisy

The flat lazy daisy is done like the lazy daisy, but with the ribbon flat as it's stitched. This stitch is often used for an iris or tulip leaf.

1 Anchor the end of the ribbon. Holding the ribbon out of the way, stitch 1/4″-1/2″ out away from the ribbon.

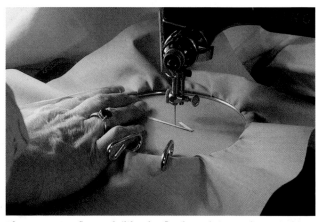

If you want a flat end (like the flat lazy daisy or fern stitch), hold the ribbon flat as you stitch it.

2 Keeping the ribbon flat, bring it over and stitch to anchor it.

3 Keeping the ribbon out of the way, stitch next to the ribbon, back to the starting point.

4 Fold the ribbon over, keeping it flat, and anchor it at the starting point. Depending on the effect desired, you may want to squish it a bit as you anchor it but keep the middle flat.

Lazy Daisy Chain

The lazy daisy chain is a running lazy daisy stitch. It is similar in looks to the chain stitch, but fuller.

1 Complete a lazy daisy stitch.

2 Stitch next to the lazy daisy, to the opposite end.

3 Fold over the ribbon and anchor it.

4 Do another lazy daisy and repeat steps 2 and 3. Continue in this way, making a chain of lazy daisies.

Double Lazy Daisy Chain

The lazy daisy chain stitch is an excellent choice for a crazy quilt stitch. To make it even more luxurious, try the double lazy daisy chain.

1 Use two colors of 2mm or 4mm ribbon. Make a lazy daisy chain by starting with a lazy daisy stitch.

2 Stitch through the middle of the lazy daisy to the outer point.

3 Fold over the ribbons, keeping them flat, and anchor them.

4 Continue making double lazy daisy stitches to the desired length.

Ribbon Stitch

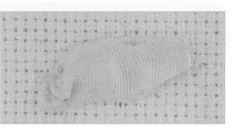

Called the ribbon stitch or straight stitch in hand embroidery, this stitch is usually done with 7mm ribbon and gives the effect of a single stitch pulled through the fabric with the ribbon held flat as it's stitched. For more delicate work, try it with 4mm ribbon.

1 Start with the end of the ribbon anchored as shown, with the end pointing toward where the petal or leaf will be. Hold the ribbon squished together as you stitch it.

2 Stitch 1/4″-3/8″ away to the other end of the petal or leaf.

3 Fold the ribbon over so it covers the cut end and carry it to the end of the stitching.

4 To finish, cut the ribbon, leaving about 1/4″. Using your tweezers, tuck the end under the flower petal and stitch it in place. These petals are independent, not connected together, and are good when you need spaced out stitches.

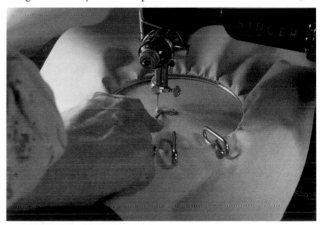

To finish most stitches, tuck the end of the ribbon under the stitch you have formed and tack it in place.

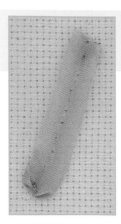

Oversewn Ribbon Stitch

The oversewn ribbon stitch is formed just like the ribbon stitch, but when done, stitch from one end to the other. This forms the center vein of a leaf or flower petal and also adds stability to a garment that will be washed frequently.

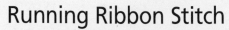

Running Ribbon Stitch

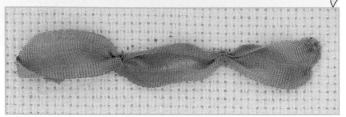

Similar to the ribbon stitch but worked in a continuing row, the running ribbon stitch is best used with wider ribbons like 7mm and 9mm.

① Begin the ribbon like you did for the ribbon stitch and anchor it in place.

② Using the tweezers to hold the ribbon in place, squish it and tack it in place.

③ Stitch forward 1/4″-1/2″. Repeat step 2 to the desired length.

Fern Stitch

The fern stitch can be used to make leaves, baskets, trellises, etc. This is a name we came up with because we used it to make ferns and it doesn't closely resemble any traditional hand stitch. It is an excellent stitch to use any time you want to fill a large area.

① Anchor the end of the ribbon as shown, keeping it flat.

② Holding the ribbon out of the way, stitch out 3/8″.

③ Bring the ribbon over, keeping it flat, and stitch across it to anchor. Stitch back to the starting point, keeping the ribbon out of the way.

④ Bring the ribbon over, keeping it flat as shown, and anchor it (think of folding it back and forth accordion style).

⑤ Continue in this manner until you've covered the desired area.

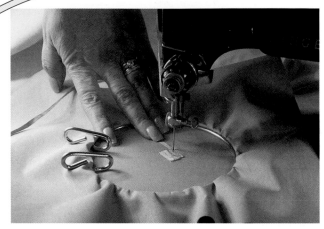

For the fern stitch, stitch the ribbon back and forth accordion style.

Oversewn Fern Stitch

Sometimes for effect or because the ribbon covers a large expanse, we oversew the fern stitch, which simply means we straight stitch back over the completed fern stitch. In the case of the pumpkins on our fall grapevine wreath, it created the look of the vertical lines that form the essence of the pumpkin.

Loose Fern Stitch

The loose fern stitch is a variation of the traditional fern stitch, using two ribbons simultaneously. Stitch the same as the fern stitch, but keep one ribbon rather taut and allow the other to be much looser. This results in a nice three-dimensional texture.

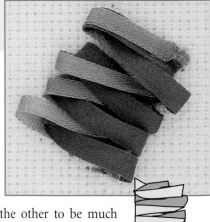

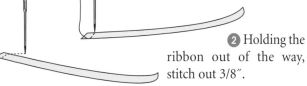

Looped Fern Stitch

1 Tack two colors of ribbon at the starting position. Carry both along the same way the fern stitch is constructed.

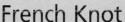

2 Using tweezers, create a loop to one side and tack it in the center.

3 Pull a loop to the other side, again tacking it in the middle. Always leave one ribbon looser than the other to give the effect of feathers or leaves or just interesting dimension.

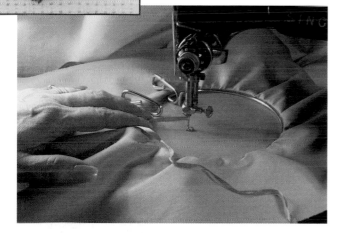

French Knot

Now we are going to do some French knots. They're easy!

When making French knots and bullion stitches, wrap the ribbon around the needle.

1 Anchor the end of the ribbon. With the needle down, wind the ribbon around the needle about three times. Keep the ribbon tension medium—not too tight or loose. The size of the French knot is determined by

the width of the ribbon and the number of times you wrap it around the needle.

2 Holding the wrapped ribbon in place with tweezers, stitch outside the knot to anchor it. You may be more comfortable sewing this stitch by turning the hand wheel by hand. French knots are often done in clusters. Try doing a couple together.

Loose French Knot

A looser, more relaxed version of the traditional French knot, the loose French knot makes an excellent bud or portion of a flower.

1 Twist the ribbon around the needle three to four times as you did for the French knot.

2 Let the ribbon relax so it's about 1/8″ from the needle.

3 Tack in place as you did the regular French knot.

Bullion Stitch

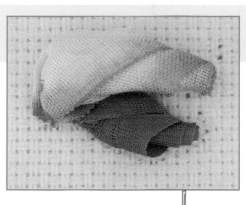

The bullion stitch is most commonly used to make rosebuds. It is done exactly like the French knot with two exceptions. Use 7mm ribbon and wrap it six times around the needle instead of three times.

1 After you've wrapped the ribbon, raise the needle by hand and move it slightly to one side. Flip the bullion over on its side and take a few stitches to anchor it. You can also spread the ribbon a bit, opening the bud before you take the anchoring stitches.

Ruching

Ruching is traditionally done by hand by gathering the ribbon down the center and then applying it to the fabric. We gather as we go.

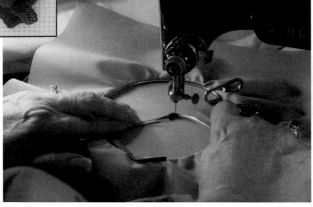

For ruching or the loop stitch, hold the ribbon in your left hand and pull a loop of ribbon with the tweezers to the right.

❶ Anchor the end of the ribbon and hold it out to the left with your left hand. With the tweezers, pull about 1/4″ ribbon to the right of the needle. Take a stitch or two to anchor and repeat.

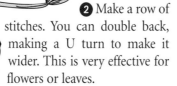

❷ Make a row of stitches. You can double back, making a U turn to make it wider. This is very effective for flowers or leaves.

Single-Edged Ruching

Very pretty morning glory type flowers can be made by ruching only the edge of 7mm, 10mm, or 13mm wide ribbon.

❶ You will always be sewing in the center of the flower. Start by folding the end of the ribbon under 1/4″ and anchoring it flat as shown.

❷ Hold a pleat in place with tweezers and stitch.

❸ Continue, pulling another pleat and stitching, working in a circle until you've completed a flower.

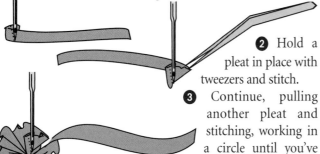

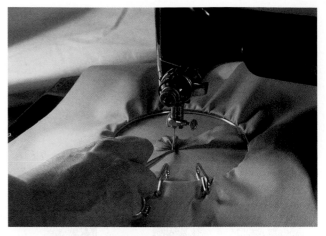

Single-edged ruching takes little tucks at the edge of the ribbon.

Edge Tucked Single-Edged Ruching

This stitch evolved when we began working with the very wide (25mm and 40mm) ribbons. They were so wide, they needed to be corralled a bit. Stitch the flowers the same as when doing single-edged ruching and then go back and bunch the ribbon up in a few places and tack it in place. You may want to add a bead in this tack as well.

Couching

In some respects, all the stitches we've done could be called couching. The term couching means tacking a surface ribbon or thread in place instead of threading it in the sewing machine. We couch certain threads or ribbons to make stems or tree branches.

❶ Anchor the end of the ribbon by tucking it under and stitching it in place. In the case of yarns or threads, just stitch over the end without tucking it under.

❷ Stitch next to the ribbon, jumping onto the ribbon occasionally to tack it down.

Couching-With-a-Twist

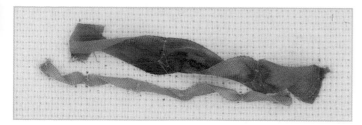

This is a nice rambling stitch, useful if you are doing a free form or meandering design. It's also very pretty on lettering.

1 Anchor the end by tucking it under. Stitch 1/4″, keeping the ribbon out of the way.

2 Twist the ribbon 1/2 turn and anchor it.

3 Continue to the desired length.

Twisted Stem Stitch

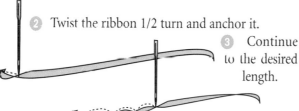

1 To sew a twisted stem stitch, anchor the ribbon at the end and twist the ribbon with your fingers.

2 Couch the ribbon in place.

Loosely Twisted Stitch

The loosely twisted stitch is formed like the twisted stem stitch, but left much looser. Anchor at the end of the ribbon (4mm or 7mm), twist it gently, and tack in place.

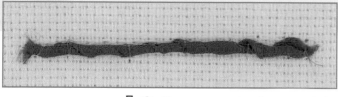

Connecting Stitch

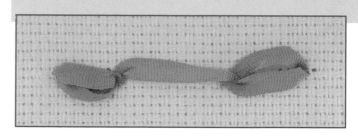

The connecting stitch is formed by simply carrying the ribbon from one stitch to another, as in a branch connecting two leaves. Here we've shown it between two lazy daisies. Stitch to where you want to go and then bring the ribbon over and tack it in place.

Coil Stitch

The coil stitch is used with metallic cords or boucle type cords or yarns. Begin in the center and simply couch the cord in a coiled shape as shown.

Loop Stitch

The loop stitch is similar to ruching and makes a pretty flower.

1 Anchor at the edge of the ribbon. Hold the ribbon in your left hand and pull a loop to the right with tweezers. Stitch to anchor.

2 Continue pulling loops, making a circle and always anchoring the loops in the same spot in the center.

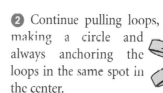

Running Loop Stitch

By making a row of loops instead of a circle, you can do a very pretty cascading type flower or three-dimensional leaves and foliage. Do exactly as you did with the looped flower, but work in a row instead of the center.

Running Loop Stitch Topped With Another Ribbon

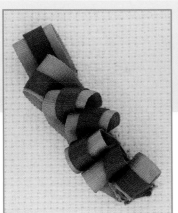

If you work the running loop stitch with two contrasting ribbon colors in two different widths (7mm and 4mm, for example) at the same time, you will create a beautiful two-color design. We did cascading flowers and yummy ribbon Christmas candy!

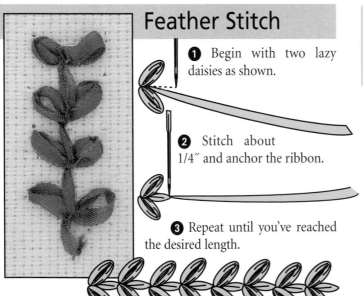

Feather Stitch

❶ Begin with two lazy daisies as shown.

❷ Stitch about 1/4″ and anchor the ribbon.

❸ Repeat until you've reached the desired length.

Half Feather Stitch

The half feather stitch is done like the regular feather stitch, but you only do one lazy daisy stitch each time, alternating sides. You can get different looks by keeping the ribbon flat rather than scrunched.

Blanket Stitch

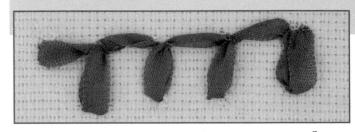

❶ Begin with a flat lazy daisy as shown.

❷ Stitch 1/4″, anchor the ribbon, and repeat step 1. Repeat from there.

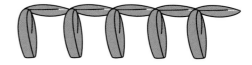

Angled Blanket Stitch

This is a nice variation of the blanket stitch, created with the stitches at an angle instead of straight out.

Zigzag Stitch

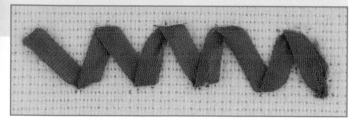

① The zigzag stitch is easy! Start by anchoring the end of the ribbon and stitch 1/4″ at an angle as shown.

② Keeping it flat, bring the ribbon over and anchor it.

③ Stitch at an angle, then fold the ribbon accordion style and tack it in place. Think of it as a stretched out fern stitch. Repeat to the desired length.

Cross Stitch

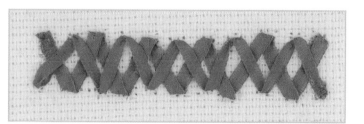

① The cross stitch is done like the zigzag stitch, but twice. Start by stitching a row of zigzags, keeping some distance between them.

② Using a different color (if desired), sew back down the row with another row of zigzags.

Pistol Stitch

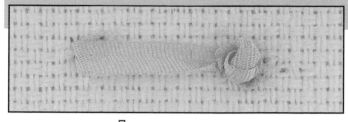

① Tack down the end of the ribbon at the starting point.

② Stitch straight up 1/4″-1/2″, bring the ribbon up, and stitch to anchor, keeping the ribbon flat.

③ Make a French knot at the end. Without cutting the ribbon, stitch back to the starting point. Anchor the ribbon here.

④ Repeat steps 2 and 3 at a 45 degree angle (if desired).

⑤ Stitch 1/4″-1/2″ away and repeat steps 1 through 4 for another set of pistol stitches, until the desired length is completed.

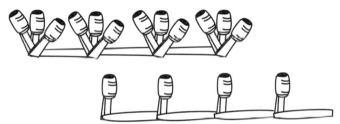

Chain French Knots

① Anchor 2mm or 4mm ribbon and make a French knot.

② Stitch about 1/4″-1/2″ away and anchor the ribbon.

③ Make a French knot and repeat steps 2 and 3 until you've completed the desired length.

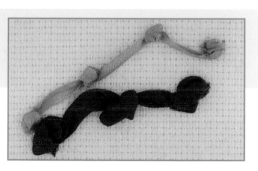

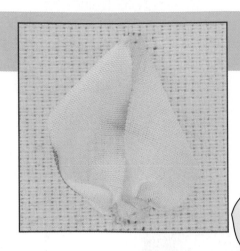

Calla Lily Stitch

Named for the flower of the same name, the calla lily stitch is a matter of tacking the ribbon in a loop formed as shown. We usually use 7mm ribbon.

When you're ready to apply a bead, take your foot off the foot control/pedal. Place the bead on the fabric near where you want to sew it on. Turn the hand wheel by hand and insert just the tip of the needle in the bead.

Move it gently to where you want it and turn the wheel by hand toward you to complete a stitch. Take an additional stitch one bead's width away. This will cause the bead to pop over on its side.

Basic Beading

Beads add glamour, highlights, and just plain fun to ribbon embroidery. In the past you may have sewn them on by hand—now you can do it by machine!

But first things first. When you buy beads, be sure that a **threaded** sewing machine needle will fit into the bead. Take one with you to the store because it's hard to guess. We worked with size 6/0 and 8/0 beads by Gick. You may or may not be able to find these or you may already have beads. Any beads will work as long as a threaded sewing machine needle can be inserted into the bead. The smallest sewing machine needle available is size 8/60. Use it for smaller beads.

One other caution is that long bugle beads (long and skinny tubular beads) won't work very well. Generally you want round or short squarish ones as shown.

Apply the beads at the same time as the ribbon embroidery. It's faster and easier because you are already there and the threads are securely anchored.

Chapter 4

Spring
Projects

Spring Flowers Grapevine Wreath

Supplies

16″ square of natural color linen or linen-like fabric

Yarn: 4-ply knitting yarn, macramé yarn, or cotton cords in several muted shades of brown for the wreath

4mm ribbon: lavender, medium purple, dark purple, hand-dyed variegated purple, mauve, plum, pink, pale peach, peach, spring green, olive green, medium yellow, hand-dyed variegated yellow

7mm ribbon: red, pink, hand-dyed variegated purple, olive green

Beads: cobalt blue, yellow

Air-soluble marker or chalk

Liquid fabric stiffener

Grapevine wreaths are a wonderful blank canvas for any season of the year. For your Spring Wreath, think of the moist black earth surrounding the first green shoots from the bulbs that have been dormant all winter long, awaiting the warmth of the ever-lengthening days of spring! Think of the delicate pastels, the tiny fragile blossoms, followed on a daily basis by tulips, jonquils, and daffodils along with all the blooming trees—magnolias, lilacs, forsythia, the apple blossoms!

Think yellows, pinks, purples, soft peaches, lavenders, and the pale bluish purples of grape hyacinths.

❶ Draw a 6″ circle (or whatever size you prefer) on the fabric with an air-soluble marker or chalk. Choose several shades and thicknesses of muted brown yarns and cords and couch them over the circle, creating a wreath about 1″ wide. Intertwine them as you go, pulling them under the previous strands with the tweezers. Try stitching several strands down at once, twisting them as you go.

❷ Let's begin our decorations with the peonies. Using 4mm plum and pink ribbons, begin at the top of the flower with four lazy daisy stitches in a row. Move down and do another row below the first. Alternate between the pink and plum by stitching several lazy daisies of one color, bring in another color and do several more lazy daisies, then return to the original color. Alternate the two colors until the peony is complete. Continue stitching until you have three or four rows of petals. Make the stems with 4mm spring green using the twisted stem stitch. Add several lazy daisy leaves with 4mm spring green ribbon.

❸ In the upper left, stitch several irises with 7mm hand-dyed variegated purple ribbon. Stitch one lazy daisy straight up and two going down on an angle. Stitch a French knot in the center with 4mm lavender.

❹ Below the irises, stitch several red tulips and a pink one with 7mm ribbon. Simply do three lazy daisies for each tulip. Add an olive green twisted stem stitch stem and several leaves of 7mm olive green. Sew them with an elongated flat lazy daisy. Add a red and hand-dyed variegated purple tulip side-by-side on the lower right. Embellish with a leaf or two as above.

❺ Stitch four apple blossoms with 4mm pale peach and peach, using the lazy daisy stitch. Stitch the stems and leaves with 4mm olive green, using the lazy daisy stitch.

❻ No spring bouquet is complete without lilacs. Using all the purples and lilacs, stitch a variety of French knots. Use different ribbon colors and shades, as well as different widths to give them a nice texture. It will be so realistic, you'll swear you can smell the lovely lilac fragrance!

❼ Use a hand-dyed variegated 4mm yellow intermixed with 4mm medium yellows to do the ruching stitch and create lovely forsythia.

❽ Create a handful of grape hyacinths with clustered cobalt blue beads.

❾ To make the curly tendrils, wrap some brown yarn around a large knitting needle or wooden dowel. Stiffen with fabric stiffener and let dry. Remove and cut into 1″ sections. Pull apart slightly and tack in place.

❿ The wreath can be mounted on stretcher bars and framed (as ours was) or made into a pillow or wall hanging. Keep in mind that the curly tendrils can't be washed or dry cleaned, so leave them off a project that will require cleaning.

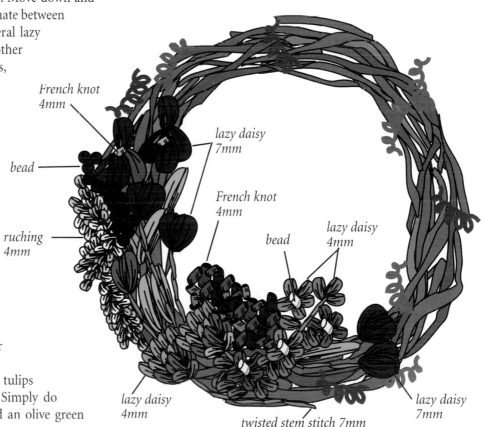

French knot 4mm

lazy daisy 7mm

bead

French knot 4mm

ruching 4mm

bead

lazy daisy 4mm

lazy daisy 4mm

lazy daisy 7mm

twisted stem stitch 7mm

*N*othing deserves more acclaim than the announcement of a new baby! Make a wonderful memento for new parents by framing a copied or re-created birth announcement.

❶ If you have a computer, scan the birth announcement or re-create it and print it out on computer printer fabric. If you don't have a computer, take the announcement and photo transfer paper to a copy shop and have them "mirror image" the type so it doesn't come out backwards. Iron the photo transfer paper on fabric according to the manufacturer's directions. You now have an announcement, ready to embellish.

❷ Set the machine for ribbon embroidery according to the directions on page 9. Start with the lavender double carnation at the top. To create the double carnation, use the single-edged ruching stitch with 13mm lavender edge-dyed

Quick Project
Framed Birth Announcement

Supplies

Birth announcement, copy, or
   computer re-creation
Single or double pre-cut mat
Frame
Computer printer fabric by
   June Tailor or photo transfer
   paper by Quiltmakers
4mm ribbon: pale green
7mm ribbon: pale green, pale
   blue, lavender, variegated
   pastel
13mm edge-dyed ribbon:
   lavender, pink, blue, yellow

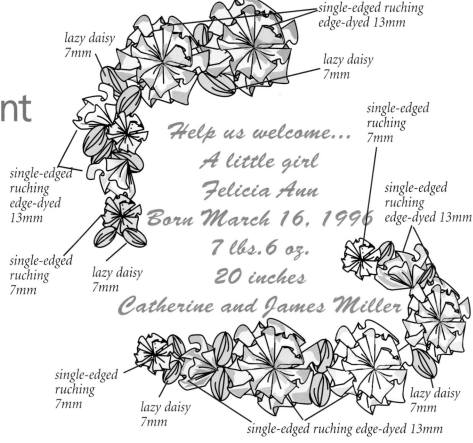

*single-edged ruching
edge-dyed 13mm*

*lazy daisy
7mm*

*lazy daisy
7mm*

*single-edged
ruching
7mm*

*single-edged
ruching
edge-dyed
13mm*

*single-edged
ruching
edge-dyed 13mm*

*single-edged
ruching
7mm*

*lazy daisy
7mm*

*Help us welcome...
A little girl
Felicia Ann
Born March 16, 1996
7 lbs. 6 oz.
20 inches
Catherine and James Miller*

*single-edged
ruching
7mm*

*lazy daisy
7mm*

*lazy daisy
7mm*

single-edged ruching edge-dyed 13mm

ribbon. The 13mm ribbon gives a delightfully full effect for dimensional projects. Start by creating a basic single-edged ruching flower as described on page 16. Continue for one or two more rounds.

❸ Working counter clockwise, stitch the pink carnation below the same way with 13mm pink edge-dyed ribbon.

❹ The pale yellow bud is stitched with the 13mm yellow edge-dyed ribbon. Stitch 1/2 the basic single-edge ruched flower, then stop.

Tuck the ribbon under. Meet the starting edge and hold it out of the way with tweezers, then tack it in place.

❺ Stitch the pale blue bud the same and continue with the 7mm single-edged ruching stitch flowers.

❻ Fill in with the pale green leaves in both 4mm and 7mm ribbon.

❼ Complete the remainder of the design following the diagram. Remember - you will need to adjust the position of the flowers to fit the lettering on the announcement.

Quick Project
Note Card

*M*ake a very special note card as a handwritten announcement or special thank you. Even though we created this one with a new baby in mind, they are suitable for any occasion—graduation, birthday, wedding, anniversary, or holiday greeting. Choose your favorite flowers and go for it!

❶ Stitching on paper is no problem at all if you find a paper stable enough to be sewn without a hoop. Tissue paper won't work and typing/copy paper is close but still too lightweight. This note card is approximately the same weight as most greeting cards or index cards. When sewing on paper, use a minimum of stitches. Too many, too close together will perforate the paper and make it unstable.

❷ Choose the flower(s) you want from the Birth Announcement project and follow the directions and stitch diagram for that flower. Try our design first, then add your favorite flowers or critters. Just remember that you don't hoop the card and that you'll use tweezers to hold everything in place.

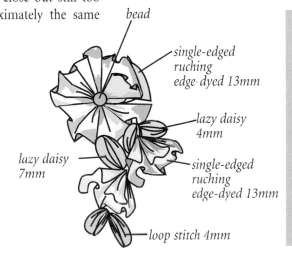

bead

single-edged ruching edge-dyed 13mm

lazy daisy 4mm

lazy daisy 7mm

single-edged ruching edge-dyed 13mm

loop stitch 4mm

Supplies

Blank note cards available at art supply or craft stores

13mm edge-dyed ribbon: pink, blue, purple

7mm ribbon: pale green

4mm ribbon: pale green

1 yellow bead

April

Spring Sweater

Supplies

Lightweight sweater (silk, cotton, rayon, or a blend)
Adhesive stabilizer (so you don't need to hoop the sweater)
2mm silk ribbon: yellow
4mm silk ribbon: bright green, grayed green, gold, mauve, pink, flesh, brown, dark orange
7mm silk ribbon: edge-dyed yellow, edge-dyed green, brown, pink
Cording: nubby white, grayed green, pink, gold several shades of brown, light yellow
Beads: 2 blue, 1 red, 2 opalescent

*S*pring! After our long cold snowy winters up here in the North, we welcome spring with open arms. We still have the chilly days where a sweater or long sleeves are needed, but just the fact that the sweater is now silk, cotton, or rayon is a welcome change from the wools that have seen us through the winter. We celebrate spring with the decorations on this sweater. Do any of these serve as reminders of spring for you?

In life, our spring may be a new birth, a new venture or career... we still need spring in our life even as we age!

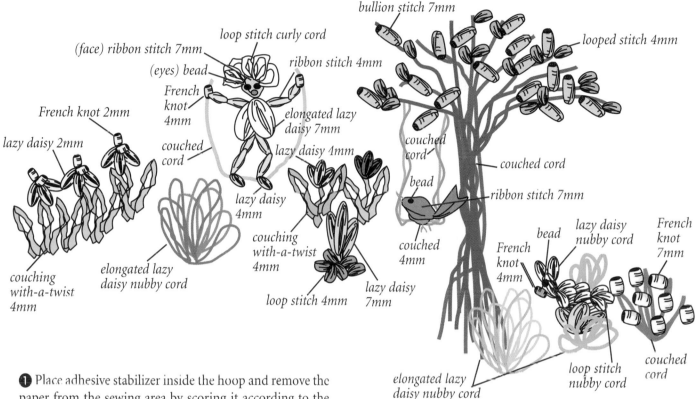

① Place adhesive stabilizer inside the hoop and remove the paper from the sewing area by scoring it according to the manufacturer's directions.

② Try on the sweater and mark the area for embroidery with chalk or an air-soluble marker. You will work the pattern from left to right. Fit as large an area as possible into the hoop. (Hint: When you've finished working one area of the sweater and are ready to move to another, you don't need to replace the entire piece of stabilizer, just patch the hole area.)

③ Start with the daffodils. With 4mm bright green ribbon, work some couched stems and several couching-with-a-twist leaves. Top with 2mm yellow flowers made using three lazy daisy stitches and two French knots in the top portion and center of the flower.

④ The small bush is made with nubby cording in grayed green and dark brown. Begin at the bottom of the bush and stitch up 1/2"-1", carrying the cording up. These are elongated lazy daisies made carrying two cords at once. Finish it with a couple loop stitched branches to give it dimension.

⑤ Next is the little rope skipper. Start by sketching a stick figure of the girl (or boy) on the stabilizer. Stitch legs and arms with a ribbon stitch of 4mm flesh ribbon, pinched together at the joints. The feet are made with small lazy daisy stitches. The hands are made with a small French knot. The jump rope is couched pink shiny cord with frayed ends, as a jump rope might be. The bubble suit is two elongated lazy daisy stitches formed with 7mm edge-dyed yellow ribbon. Begin at the neck and make two stitches down. Make the face with 7mm pink in a ribbon stitch. Attach the bead eyes and mouth. The nice curls are made using a curly yellow cord and making loop stitches around her face. Isn't she a cute little one?

⑥ The tulips are made with 4mm gold and mauve ribbon. Make one vertical lazy daisy stitch and two at 45 degree angles next to it. The stems are couching-with-a-twist, as are the leaves.

⑦ The patch of light green grass is made with 7mm edge-dyed light green ribbon. Loosely twist the ribbon in a lazy daisy stitch. The ground is a small 4mm brown loop stitch.

8 The tree is several colors of brown cording couched together for the trunk and spread slightly for the roots. The branches are separated, spread, and couched randomly. The leaves are randomly placed bullions made with 7mm edge-dyed green ribbon. Add loop-stitched pink buds just starting to open with 4mm pink ribbon. The rope swing is gold cord twisted slightly and couched. The curious little robin is made with a ribbon stitch of 7mm brown. Leave the tail free to give the tail feathers dimension. The robin's breast is a small piece of couched dark orange ribbon peeking out of the body. The beak and feet are a small piece of gold ribbon couched in position. Sew the beaded eye on at the same time as the beak.

9 The bush below the tree is done the same as the bush is step 4.

10 The playful little bunny is nestled in the grass watching the entire scene. Sketch the small body shape and fill it with a nubby white cord in a loop stitch. The bunny's ears are lazy daisy stitches. The nose is 4mm pink ribbon in a tight French knot. Attach a bead for the eye. Make the bush the bunny is hiding in the same as in step 4.

11 The forsythia bush is couched brown cord with blossoms made with 7mm edge-dyed yellow ribbon worked into a French knot.

*E*aster has many meanings and traditions that differ from family to family and year to year. Easter eggs have emerged through the centuries as a symbol of Easter. From the beautiful European masterpieces made from real egg shells, china, crystal, or gold to the "hand-dyed with love" masterpieces created by the kids, all have their place in our lives. You can create an heirloom to be treasured and passed down through the generations with a few bits and pieces of fabric, trim, ribbon, beads, and a lowly Styrofoam egg!

Quick Project
Fabergé Easter Egg

Supplies

Styrofoam egg (The one shown is 3½″ x 5″ and was labeled 3½″ at the store. Don't worry about the size, we'll tell you how to make a pattern for whatever size egg you purchase.)

1/8 yard pale yellow damask or similar tone-on-tone pastel fabric

1 yard 1/2″-wide braid or trim to match or contrast fabric

Fabric glue

Pins (without plastic heads)

13mm ribbon: edge-dyed pale blue, lavender, pink, yellow

7mm ribbon: grass green, over-dyed pastel, lavender

4mm ribbon: lavender

Beads: yellow

2 rubber bands

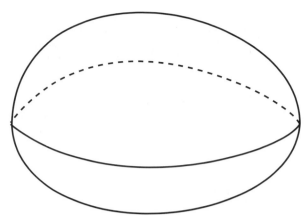

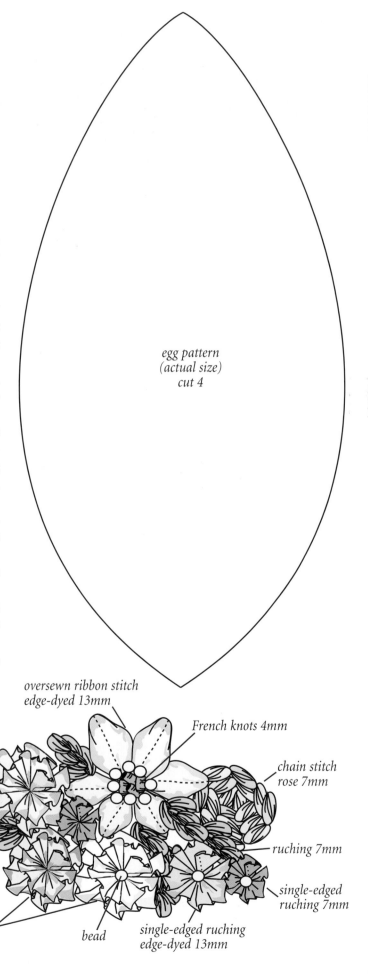

egg pattern
(actual size)
cut 4

❶ Make a paper pattern for the egg if it differs from ours. Place the rubber bands as shown above, dividing the egg into four parts.

❷ Cut the pattern from scrap fabric and try it on the egg. If it doesn't fit, make your own pattern on scrap fabric by pinning it on one segment of the divided egg. You don't need seam allowances because the segments will butt together and be covered with braid.

❸ Trace the pattern on the pastel fabric, leaving enough excess fabric to fit into the hoop. This is where you'll do the ribbon embroidery.

❹ Following the diagram, stitch the double carnations with 13mm edge-dyed pastel ribbons, using the single-edged ruching stitch. Begin with a single flower, stitching around the circle, but instead of ending it, continue several more rounds to create a multi-layered flower.

❺ Stitch the focal point blossom with the oversewn ribbon stitch in 13mm edge-dyed blue ribbon and finish the center with 4mm lavender French knots and beads.

❻ The rose is sewn with 7mm pastel over-dyed ribbon using the chain stitch.

❼ Fill in with several lavender flowers, created with 7mm ribbon and the single-edged ruching stitch. Embellish with a yellow bead in the center of each.

❽ Complete the design with 7mm grass green ribbon, stitched with the ruching stitch.

❾ Remove the embroidered fabric from the hoop and center the pattern over the embroidery. Cut one piece from the embroidered fabric and three pieces from unembroidered fabric. Place the fabric pieces on the egg and pin in place.

❿ Cut the braid into segments long enough to cover the four joints.

⓫ Using fabric glue, glue the braid in place to cover the joints. Secure with pins until the glue dries.

oversewn ribbon stitch
edge-dyed 13mm

French knots 4mm

single-edged
ruching
edge-dyed
13mm

chain stitch
rose 7mm

ruching
7mm

ruching 7mm

single-edged
ruching 7mm

single-edged ruching
edge-dyed 13mm

bead

single-edged ruching
edge-dyed 13mm

Mother/Daughter Dresses

May

Supplies

Simple pattern for dresses
Denim/chambray fabric
(amount called for in
pattern)
1 yard chambray blue and white
striped shirting for binding
Purple buttons (or your favorite
color)

W ithout a doubt, mothers and daughters share a special bond. They share interests that Dad and brothers just aren't into. Even as toddlers, little girls love to dress up like Mom. A special mother/daughter outfit can create lasting memories well beyond childhood. Marie's memory is of navy blue cotton dresses with big white buttons and collars. Betty's is bright yellow t-shirt dresses worn by Mom and three older daughters.

Our denim/chambray dresses are made from a simple beginner's pattern but could be any clothing item, such as matching ready-made denim shirts, sweatshirts, or t-shirts. Choose your favorite "hanging-out" clothes and go for it.

Do a few designs or go all out with your favorites. We chose fruits and veggies for Mom, because gardening is her favorite hobby. Our little girl wanted her favorite woodland creatures.

Don't forget our Quick Project - hats to keep the summer sun at bay. It's a great way to try out a new design!

In addition to the embroidery, we've added great tips for applying bias binding. It's fast, easy, and all machine done. Let's go!

Sew the Dresses

❶ Sew both the dresses, following the pattern directions. When you get to the facings, apply them **wrong sides together**. Stitch the seamline with 5/8″ seam allowance and trim it to 1/4″.

❷ Apply the bias binding as follows. Cut 2″-wide binding strips on the bias. Join several strips to make sufficient length to go up the front, around the back, and down the other front. Fold in half lengthwise with wrong sides together and press. Be careful not to stretch the fabric.

❸ Place the binding on the wrong side of the area to be bound, with the raw edges even, and stitch in place.

wrong side

❹ Bring the binding around to the front side, folding it in half. Use the original stitching line as shown to line it up. Press.

right side

❺ Choose a blanket stitch or blind hem stitch if you have it, or use a small zigzag to stitch the binding in place.

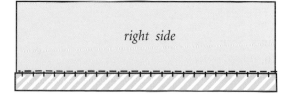

right side

Ribbon Embroidery for Mom's Dress

*M*ake your own "recipe" by adding or substituting your favorite fruits and vegetables, spices, and flavorings.

❶ We're ready to embroider! Divide the top front in four sections and mark it off with chalk or an air-soluble marker. The left side has grapes in the top section, carrots next, then a sunflower and finishes with several pumpkins. The right side has corn and a basket of strawberries in the top section. Below are peppers and mushrooms, then pea pods, and below them onions. Sketch in the approximate shapes.

❷ Make the grapes using French knots and all your scraps of purples. We used 7mm ribbons, but don't hesitate to mix in some 4mm too. Stitch the leaves using 7mm and 10mm ribbons and the fern stitch. End with the cord, using the chain stitch, bringing the ends up into the leaves to create veining. Couch the veins in place, adding in extra pieces of cord as needed.

❸ Add pale orange carrots with elongated ribbon stitches. (When you elongate the ribbon stitch, it's a good idea to stitch the ribbon down on each edge.) Add flat lazy daisy carrot tops with 2mm medium green.

❹ Begin the sunflower with a circle of lazy daisies. Mix and match 4mm golds and yellows for texture and interest. Fill the center with French knots using some 4mm and some 7mm ribbons of varying browns and blacks. Add a twisted stem stitch stem and some oversewn ribbon stitch leaves.

❺ Use the fern stitch to create the pumpkins with 7mm rust/orange over-dyed with plum ribbon. An elongated oversewn ribbon stitch makes a nice stem.

❻ Pull it all together with a vine. Draw a stem, following our design or adapting it as you like, and add leaves using all the 7mm green ribbons. (This is a great learning experience for combining all the greens of nature, even though

Supplies

2mm ribbon: medium green, dark green, light brown
4mm ribbon: dark brown, black, reddish brown, taupe, light yellow, medium yellow, dark yellow, gold
7mm ribbon: blue/green hand-dyed variegated, light green, dark green, medium green, olive green, light green hand-dyed variegated, lavender, medium purple, dark purple, dark purple hand-dyed variegated, pale orange, rust/orange over-dyed with plum, black, brown, taupe, dark red, light red, yellow, ivory, over-dyed beige-on-beige
Cottonaire textured purples
Cords: olive green, dark green

they clash when looked at individually. Study the leaves in nature - they range from the blue greens of evergreens to the yellow greens of ferns. They constantly change with the seasons and never clash!) We used the oversewn ribbon stitch and a couched cord. If you don't have many 7mm greens, try 4mm greens using the lazy daisy stitch.

7 Now on to the right side. Make the corn with French knots in a variety of yellows and golds. We used 4mm ribbons, but a few large kernels of 7mm wouldn't be out of line. Add green husks with 7mm green, using an elongated ribbon stitch and stitching down the center for stability.

8 Make the strawberry basket using 4mm taupe ribbon. Construct the basket shape with the fern stitch. Then use the tweezers or thread the ribbon into a large blunt hand needle and weave it back in the other direction. Tack it in place at the end. Add the strawberries with 7mm dark red ribbon, using the ribbon stitch. The stems are 2mm dark green flat lazy daisy stitches.

9 A bounty of peppers add color and texture with 7mm

ribbons in medium green, yellow, and light red. Use the fern stitch and stitch back through the center of the ribbon for added stability and texture. End with 2mm green stems using the flat lazy daisy stitch.

10 We threw in some mushrooms for flavor. Stitch the stems first with a flat lazy daisy stitch so the ends will be covered by the mushrooms. Use 7mm ivory ribbon and the ribbon stitch for the mushroom tops. Keep the bottom flat and "squish" the top for proper mushroom shapes.

11 Start the pea pods with the pod. Choose a 7mm green and lay an elongated ribbon stitch in place, the length of the pod. Fill it with 7mm French knots, using all the available greens.

12 No pot is complete without onions! The over-dyed beige-on-beige gives just a hint of color on an ivory based ribbon. Stitch the fern stitch and complete the tops using an elongated oversewn ribbon stitch with 7mm green.

13 Tie the design together with a wandering vine with a couched cord stem and oversewn ribbon stitch leaves of varying colors of greens.

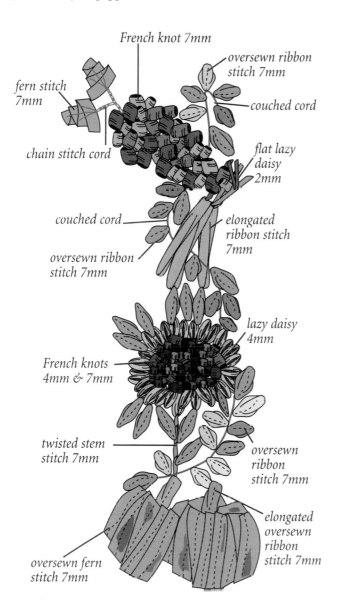

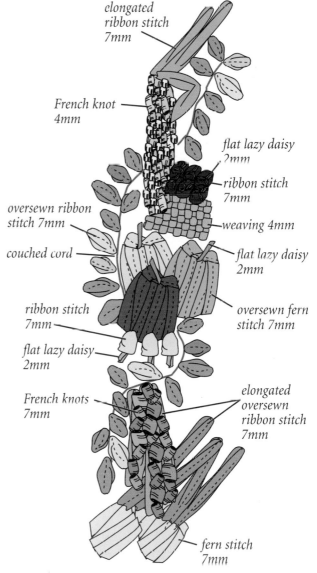

Ribbon Embroidery for Daughter's Dress

❶ Transfer the animal sketches on the next page to the fabric. You might want to use dressmaker's carbon paper.

❷ Let's begin with the friendly skunk. He's been overwhelmed by the wonderful aroma of daisies! Using 4mm black ribbon, cover the black areas with fern stitches. Add white stripes with 2mm ribbon. As you pivot the fern stitch around the tip of his tail, think of a wagon wheel, always returning to the center as you round the curve. Add black beads for eyes.

❸ Make the leaves and grass with 2mm medium green lazy daisy stitches and the daisies with 4mm yellow. Finish with French knots stitched in 4mm white.

❹ Below the skunk resides a rrrrraaabbit, munching on a carrot. Start with 4mm beige ribbon and stitch his body with the fern stitch, continuing to complete his head. His ears are lazy daisy stitches with a bend in the middle. Finish his tail using the loop stitch. All you need is a black bead for his eye and a 4mm mauve French knot stitched for his nose. The tasty carrot is an elongated lazy daisy of 4mm orange with 2mm medium green leaves. Fill in with 2mm medium green grass and 4mm spring green lazy daisy greenery and he's done!

❺ The squirrel is so proud of his beaded acorns. Couch his shape with gray-brown yarn. Start with the outer shape and work your way to the center. Add a black bead for his eye and brown beads for the acorns. Give him a nice base of 2mm medium green grass using lazy daisy stitches and finish with 7mm red lazy daisy tulips and 2mm medium green, lazy daisy leaves.

❻ Mr. Mouse is timid, hiding under his fern but totally enjoying his snack of cheese. Start with 2mm taupe ribbon and stitch him with the fern stitch. His tail is done with twisted stem stitches. Add a black bead for his eye and a 4mm mauve French knot for his nose. Give him his cheese with 4mm yellow ribbon using the fern stitch.

❼ Add the fern using 4mm olive green ribbon and the fern

Supplies

2mm ribbon: medium green, white
  2mm cotton taupe by Mokuba
4mm ribbon: yellow, black, white, beige, spring
  green, mauve, olive green, purple, dark green
7mm ribbon: orange, red, purple, dark green,
  ivory Cottonaire by Mokuba, over-dyed
  variegated green
Yarn and cord: gray-brown yarn, olive green
  pearl rayon cord
Beads: black and green for eyes, assorted blue,
  yellow and orange for flower centers, brown
  for acorns

stitch. We added some color with 2mm green lazy daisies, forming the leaves and stem for a purple lazy daisy flower with a yellow bead center.

❽ The turtle used up all our scraps of green ribbon. Use the fern stitch to fill each segment of his shell. Add his legs using 4mm green ribbon and give him bright green beaded eyes. His greenery is stitched with 7mm dark green ribbon and the flower he's resting under is stitched with 7mm purple ribbon using the lazy daisy stitch. The center is blue beads.

❾ For the wonderful coloration on the frog use 7mm edge-dyed variegated green ribbon. Stitch the fern stitch, "squishing and squeezing" the ribbon as necessary to form his frog legs and other body parts. Add a brilliant green bead for his eye and a snippet of olive green pearl rayon for his mouth. Complete his grassy bed with 2mm medium green lazy daisy stitches and a luxurious orchid stitched with 7mm ivory lazy daisy stitches, complete with orange beads in the center.

Quick Project

Mother/
Daughter Hats

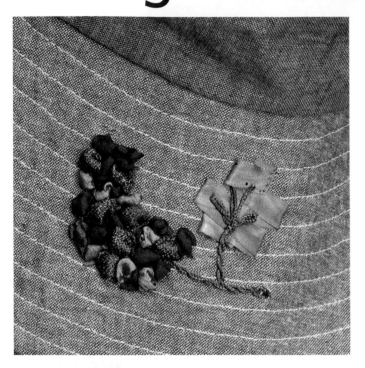

Whether you've had so much fun with the dresses you can't stop, or you're not quite ready to take on a full fledged project, our hats are a great one afternoon commitment! Mom and daughter can choose their favorite designs and complete them on a ready-made hat or one they make themselves. Mom chose grapes and daughter chose her favorite—the turtle.

Our hat pattern was a simple beginner's pattern that we embellished with extra stitching on the brim and, of course, ribbon embroidery. Refer to the dresses for stitching instructions.

Choose your favorite design—veggies, critters, or maybe a flower from another chapter. Embroider, enjoy, and wear with pride!

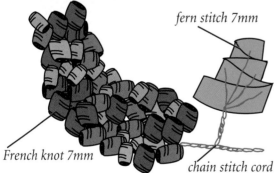

fern stitch 7mm

French knot 7mm

chain stitch cord

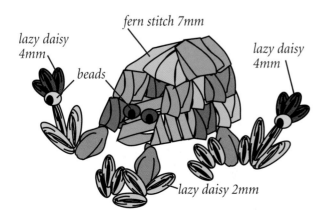

fern stitch 7mm

lazy daisy 4mm

lazy daisy 4mm

beads

lazy daisy 2mm

Chapter 5

Summer Projects

Summer Flowers Grapevine Wreath

Supplies

16″ square of natural color linen or linen-like fabric

Yarn: 4-ply knitting yarn, macramé yarn, or cotton cords in several muted shades of browns for the wreath

2mm ribbon: gold

4mm ribbon: hand-dyed variegated purple, pale blue, yellow, mulberry, gold, mauve/gold variegated, peach, green

7mm ribbon: orange, mauve, pink, pale pink, olive green

Beads: yellow

Liquid fabric stiffener

*F*or our Summer Wreath, open your mind to the long lazy days of summer, when children run and play, coming in smelling of sunshine and grass, and stay out after dinner chasing fireflies! Bees roam from flower to flower, feasting on pollen, and flowers are in full bloom, bursting with the sweet aromas of summer. The colors are incredible—from intense tiger lily orange and deep ruby red to the palest peach and off-white of roses, the profusion of bright pastels found in daisies, and the marvelous purples of larkspur.

❶ Draw a 6″ circle (or whatever size you prefer) on the fabric with an air-soluble marker or chalk. Choose several shades and thicknesses of muted brown yarns and cords and couch them over the circle, creating a wreath about 1″ wide. Intertwine them as you go, pulling them under the previous strands with tweezers. Try stitching several strands down at once, twisting them as you go.

❷ Stitch some luscious roses, starting with 7mm pale pink ribbon. Draw a 1″ circle and sew a chain stitch rose, starting with three dots in the center and working the chain stitch in a concentric circle. Work several more using 7mm pink and mauve ribbons. Add one smaller rose using 4mm peach ribbon. Fill in between the roses with lazy daisy leaves on twisted stem stitch stems, using 7mm olive green.

❸ Stitch several tiger lilies with 7mm orange ribbon, using several lazy daisy stitches. Complete the look with 2mm gold pistol stitches peeking out from between the petals. Using 7mm olive green ribbon, stitch the leaves using the lazy daisy stitch.

❹ The daisies are made with light blue and hand-dyed variegated mauve/gold ribbon. Use the lazy daisy stitch with 4mm yellow French knots in the center. Embellish the daisies with 4mm green leaves, using the lazy daisy stitch.

❺ Several stalks of purple larkspur complete our summer wreath. Create a long stalk with the twisted stem stitch, add the flowers with the various 4mm purple ribbons, using the lazy daisy stitch. Place a yellow bead at the base of each flower as you sew.

❻ To make the curly tendrils, wrap some brown yarn around a large knitting needle or wooden dowel. Stiffen with fabric stiffener and let dry. Remove and cut into 1″ sections. Pull apart slightly and tack in place.

❼ Finish the wreath as a framed picture, as we did, or a pillow or wallhanging. Our curly tendrils are not washable, so take that into account when choosing your project.

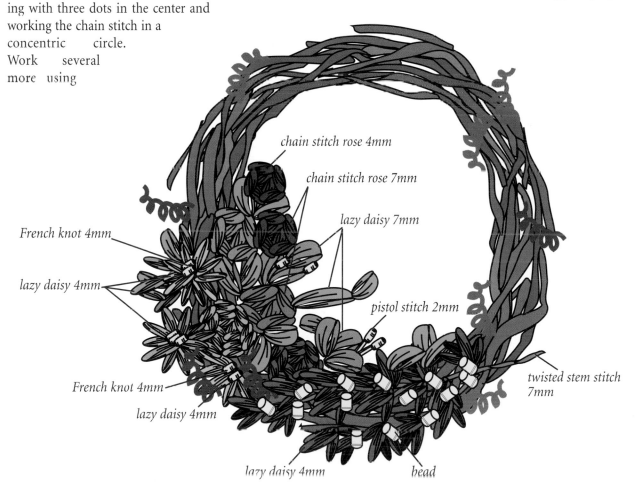

chain stitch rose 4mm

chain stitch rose 7mm

lazy daisy 7mm

French knot 4mm

lazy daisy 4mm

pistol stitch 2mm

French knot 4mm

twisted stem stitch 7mm

lazy daisy 4mm

lazy daisy 4mm

bead

Supplies

Lamp and shade
Water-soluble or tear-away
    stabilizer
Repositionable glue
2mm silk ribbon: lavender
4mm silk ribbon: bright green,
    dark olive, light taupe, light
    yellow, over-dyed
    purple/plum, mauve,
7mm silk ribbon: white, olive,
    over-dyed blue, over-dyed
    yellow, over-dyed orchid,
    taupe
13mm silk ribbon: mauve,
    edge-dyed green, edge-dyed
    gray
Boucle: brown, gray

*O*h, those first days of summer, with the sun at its finest and the colors so lush and bright, just make you want to float like the puffy clouds in the sky. We decided to make quick project "floating" ribbon embroidered designs. The finished designs are wonderful for applying anywhere you want an embellishment but would find it hard to work the embroidery in that particular spot. We attached ours with repositionable glue, but you could use permanent glue or hand stitch them on. Since this is a floating arrangement, we used loopy or loose type stitches and made certain that everything was connected to the stem or base ribbon.

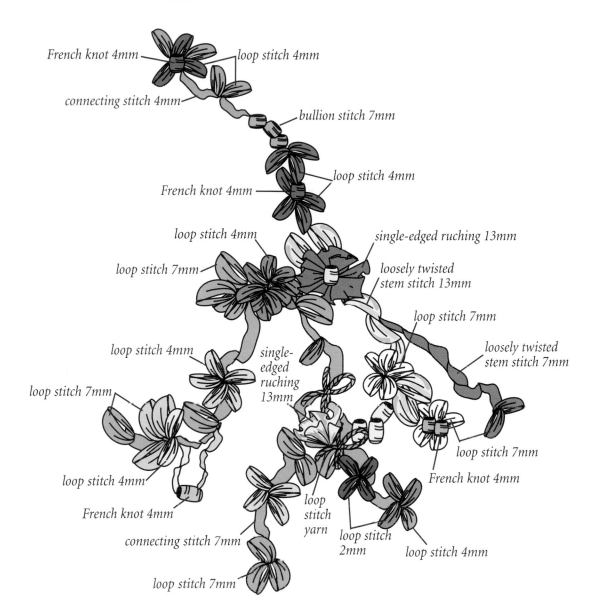

French knot 4mm — loop stitch 4mm

connecting stitch 4mm

bullion stitch 7mm

loop stitch 4mm

French knot 4mm — loop stitch 4mm

loop stitch 4mm

single-edged ruching 13mm

loop stitch 7mm

loosely twisted stem stitch 13mm

loop stitch 7mm

loosely twisted stem stitch 7mm

loop stitch 4mm

single-edged ruching 13mm

loop stitch 7mm

loop stitch 7mm

loop stitch 4mm

French knot 4mm

French knot 4mm

loop stitch yarn

connecting stitch 7mm

loop stitch 2mm

loop stitch 4mm

loop stitch 7mm

This technique works best if several 4″-5″ pieces of ribbon flowers are made before attaching, so they look like one big arrangement.

1 Place a double layer of water-soluble or tear-away stabilizer in a spring hoop. Hint: The water-soluble stabilizer dissolves when held under warm running water, but leaves the silk ribbon embroidered piece a little stiff. The tear-away stabilizer leaves "fuzzies" on the back side. Both work fine.

2 Start at the top of the design with the 4mm green leaves. Anchor the end of the ribbon on the stabilizer, make a couple loop stitches for leaves, then center with an over-dyed purple/plum looped flower. Stitch down about 1″ on the stabilizer, carrying the green ribbon and make two loop stitched leaves.

3 Continue stitching down on the stabilizer 1/2″. Work three or four bullion stitch flowers using 7mm over-dyed lavender. Attach a 4mm dark olive ribbon and work four looped leaves. Repeat the loop stitch flower using the over-dyed purple/plum ribbon and end with a loop stitch leaf. Tuck the end in and attach it with a few stitches.

4 Anchor the end of the 7mm light olive ribbon with a few stabilizing stitches. Cover this with a couple loop stitches. Make a small loop stitch flower with light lavender ribbon. Sew down on the stabilizer, then bring the 7mm avocado and give it a half twist. Stitch to anchor.

5 Follow with a loop stitch flower done in 4mm light yellow. Sew down on the stabilizer, then bring 7mm avocado and give it a half twist. Add a loop stitch leaf and continue on.

6 Sew down on the stabilizer only, bring avocado ribbon and give it a half twist. Make loop stitches with 4mm light green and 7mm taupe. Continue with two loop stitches for

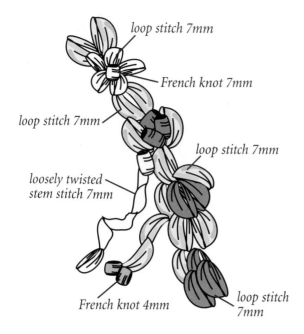

loop stitch 7mm

French knot 7mm

loop stitch 7mm

loop stitch 7mm

loosely twisted stem stitch 7mm

French knot 4mm

loop stitch 7mm

leaves. On the last one be certain to tuck the ends under.

7 Starting on top again, attach 7mm avocado ribbon, and make a looped flower with 4mm mauve. Carry the avocado under the flower and make a loop stitch leaf. Stitch the stem with a half twist and end with gray boucle in a loop stitch.

8 For the lower center branch, tack 7mm avocado on the stabilizer. Work a single-edge ruched flower with 13mm edge-dyed gray. Bring avocado ribbon around and continue down. Make a looped flower with brown pearl rayon.

9 Make another leaf, twisted stem, and then a looped flower with 2mm raspberry. Continue the stem and make a looped flower with 2mm lavender. End with looped green leaves.

10 The other branch of this section is looped 7mm avocado and 4mm yellow looped flowers.

11 The last section of the lampshade design is constructed in a similar manner. Anchor the edge of 13mm over-dyed green ribbon just under the top section and sew a loosely twisted stem stitch. Add a loop stitch flower with 7mm over-dyed yellow and end the green with several loop stitches.

12 Add some 7mm white loop stitch flowers with 4mm purple/plum French knot centers. The remaining flourish is loosely twisted 7mm over-dyed orchid.

13 The branch on the lamp base is constructed in a similar manner. Attach 7mm edge-dyed green and make several loop stitch leaves. Add a 7mm white loop stitch flower with a French knot center. Continue the 7mm green ribbon using a loosely twisted stem stitch to create the base for the remaining flowers. Add the remaining loop stitch flowers and a French knot bud.

14 Finish with a trailing tendril of 7mm over-dyed yellow ribbon, using a loosely twisted stem stitch.

15 When finished with all the pieces you need, lay the branches of flowers face down on a newspaper. Put dots of repositionable glue on all major flowers. Be certain to put a dot of glue near the top. Follow the manufacturer's instructions (ours said to allow to dry 12-24 hours), arrange in a pattern, and enjoy!

Quick Project
Embroidered Shoes

*W*e positioned a couple swags of flowers on some shoes, with repositionable glue...a fun way to dress up shoes for a special occasion. Just follow the directions for the lampshade and glue the "branches of flowers" on a pair of shoes.

Fagoted Blouse

Supplies

Tailor Tack foot for sewing machine
   (or generic equivalent)
Boat neck blouse pattern with an attached sleeve
   (no sleeve seam)
2 yards 1″-wide net trim or similar lace
Solid colored light blue cotton fabric as per pattern
   requirements
Regular weight sewing thread to match fabric
4mm ribbon: red, bright blue, variegated hand-dyed
   coral/red, variegated hand-dyed blue
7mm ribbon: light blue edge-dyed
Beads: red, blue, clear

*F*or our July project, we feature the colors of the 4th of July on a blouse. We set the fagoting in across the boat neck and continued to the end of the sleeve. You could just as easily do this with no inset sleeve. We added a 1″-wide net trim to complement the open work look. The ribbon decoration ideally reflects the fireworks of the 4th—streams of glitter and our patriotic colors. Like having fireworks exploding on the blouse! Yet the colors and fireworks are subtle enough to wear and enjoy all summer long. The lightweight fabric, net, and fagoting all give a very cool effect.

Fagoting

Fagoting is an openwork, decorative technique frequently associated with French machine sewing. It can be done whenever two seams are being joined, or where an open effect is desired. Fagoting adds an almost lace effect wherever it is inserted.

❶ A Tailor Tack foot or generic equivalent is necessary for this project. Attach the foot to your sewing machine and set the stitch width to narrow zigzag (1 or 2). Set the stitch length to a satin stitch and lower the needle tension to 1 (loose).

❷ Place two pieces of fabric to be sewn with right sides together.

❸ Begin stitching along the seam line and continue to the end.

❹ When finished, remove and pull the two layers of fabric apart firmly.

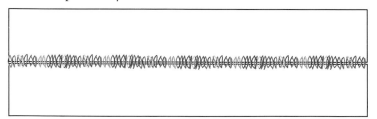

❺ Press the seam open. Reset your machine to normal tension, normal stitch length, and straight stitch.

❻ Stitch from the right side, close to the edge where the fagoting joins the fabric. This anchors the stitching and the fabric.

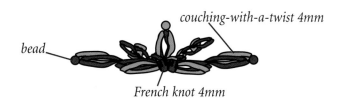

❼ We added another step to our blouse. We sewed a straight stitch down the center of the fagoting, making it cluster. It adds another pretty and different effect.

Ribbon Embroidery

❶ Follow the directions for fagoting and stitch the net trim to the blouse on each side. Lay the edge of the net trim 1/8″ over the seam allowance of the fabric. This way you'll catch the trim, but it won't all show in the fagoting. The seam allowance on the fabric will be folded back and not show through the fabric.

❷ Set the machine for a long straight stitch (4-6 stitch length) and stitch down the center of the fagoting.

❸ Follow the diagrams to complete the ribbon embroidery before you sew up the side seams. Remember to add the beads as you are doing the ribbon stitches. This makes them much more stable than if you go back in after the embroidery is complete.

couching-with-a-twist 4mm

bead

French knot 4mm

❹ Stitch the center front bow design using 4mm red and bright blue ribbon. Use the couching-with-a-twist stitch, with both ribbons simultaneously. At the outer points, add the beads. Finish with several French knots in the center of the bow.

twisted stem stitch 7mm

ruching 7mm

bead

5 On either side of the center, use 7mm light blue ribbon and stitch the ruching stitch, trailing off into a twisted stem stitch interspersed with beads along the way.

lazy daisy 4mm   loose stem stitch 4mm

bead

6 Next use 4mm variegated hand-dyed coral/red ribbon stitched in lazy daisy flowers connected by loose twisted stem stitches. Place beads in the flower centers and intersperse them randomly along the way.

loop stitch 4mm

carrying stitch 4mm   bead

7 On the outer edge, use 4mm variegated hand-dyed blue ribbon stitched with loop stitches, combined with carrying stitches. Finish with the beads.

couching-with-a-twist 4mm   bead

8 For the back of the blouse, begin in the center and form a bow with 4mm hand-dyed variegated blue ribbon with the couching-with-a-twist stitch. Place beads at the outer points as you go.

running ribbon 7mm   bead

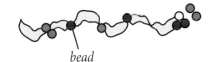

9 Working your way out, choose 7mm light blue ribbon and do the running ribbon stitch with a bead at each intersection.

couching-with-a-twist 4mm

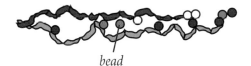

bead

10 Continue with 4mm ribbon stitched in a couching-with-a-twist stitch, with random beads placed along the way.

running ribbon 7mm

bead

11 Finish with 7mm light blue ribbon, stitched in the running ribbon stitch with beads randomly placed at the intersections.

12 Complete the blouse following the pattern directions.

*O*ur July Quick Project uses fagoting, which gives anything a cool airy look. This time we used bright summer colors, but still get the light cool look (in the Chicago area we need help to get us through the heat and humidity of summer). This little doll dress technique could be converted into a toddler dress, a lady's blouse or dress. Another way to make fagoting a part of your sewing skills.

Quick Project
18-Inch Doll Dress

Supplies

Doll dress pattern for 18″ doll (we used Sew Adorable DCC 4004)
1/2 yard batiste (or yardage called for in pattern)
Other notions called for on dress pattern
Thread: to match or contrast fagoting (we used J.P. Coats Twist thread in shades of pink, purple, and yellow)
2mm ribbon: purple, lavender, yellow, dark avocado

❶ Cut out the pattern according to the pattern directions.
❷ Cut the skirt apart 1″ above the hemline and again 2″ above the first cut.
❸ Cut the front and back collar pieces 1″ above the lower edge.

hemline

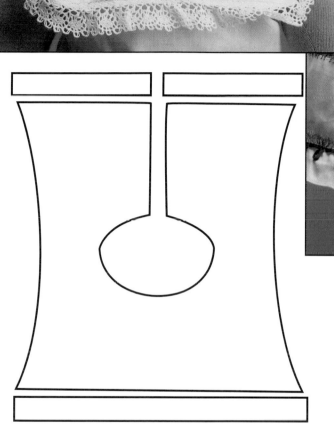

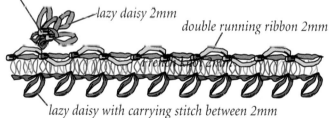

10 Working in the upper right side of the collar, add lazy daisy leaves and loop stitch in purple and lavender. Add French knot flowers.

11 Finish the dress according to the pattern directions.

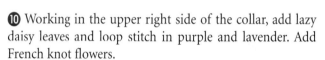

French knot 2mm
lazy daisy 2mm
double running ribbon 2mm
lazy daisy with carrying stitch between 2mm

double running ribbon 2mm
loop stitch 2mm
French knot 2mm
loop stitch 2mm
lazy daisy with carrying stitch between 2mm

4 Work fagoting according to the directions on page 44.

5 After the fagoting is complete, decorate with ribbon embroidery. Start at one edge using 2mm purple ribbon. Work the lazy daisy with a carrying stitch. Anchor the ribbon at the end, stitch approximately 1/2″, anchor the ribbon, and work a lazy daisy stitch. Repeat until you've finished the width of skirt.

6 Repeat this pattern of ribbon embroidery below the fagoting on the collar.

7 With 2mm lavender and yellow ribbon, work a double running ribbon stitch along the top row of fagoting. Anchor the end of both ribbons on the center back of the skirt. Stitch 1/2″ along the edge of the fagoting, carry the ribbons, and cross in front of the needle. Stitch over the ribbons, do a French knot, and repeat to the end of the skirt.

8 Work lazy daisy leaves with 2mm avocado ribbon between two rows of fagoting on the fabric. Position the loop stitch and French knot flower on the center front of the skirt.

9 Add the lazy daisy with French knot flowers on the two side flowers (one yellow, one lavender). These two flowers are positioned about 4″ from the center front.

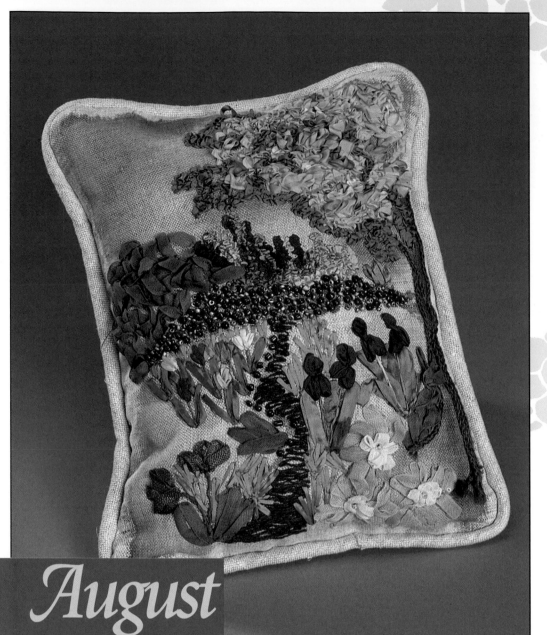

Monet Pillow

Supplies

1 yard 100% linen or
  cotton fabric
2 9″ stretcher bars
2 12″ stretcher bars
  (available at art
  supply stores)
Fabric dye (not paint—
  we used liquid
  Dye-na-Flo and
  Jacquard Textile
  Color)
Paper plates
Cotton swabs
Disposable plastic
  glasses
Push pins or thumb
  tacks

August

*T*here is a certain something in all of us that yearns to be an artist. What spurred us on was the need for even more colors of ribbon. The hundreds of solid, over-dyed, and edge-dyed colors available weren't always enough! What can we say, we could see it in our mind, but couldn't find it so "voila," we dyed it!

Actually, it's a little bit messy, but really quite easy. We'd put off dyeing for years because of visions of filling our bathtubs with dye (or, as one article suggested, filling a children's wading pool in the back yard). Needless to say, it was a bit intimidating.

Since we had the dyes out anyway, we decided to experiment with small, manageable pieces of fabric in addition to the ribbon. Our Monet pillow is the end result. Monet, of course, was the famous watercolor artist who inspired all the romantic artists throughout the centuries.

Here we outline the basic background we painted and the techniques we used. As you dye the fabric, dye some ribbons too. We primarily dyed white ribbon, but remember that over-dyed ribbons started as one color and were over-dyed with another!

Dyeing

1 Center a 13″ x 16″ piece of fabric on the stretcher bars and tack it in place with push pins or thumb tacks. Hold the fabric under running water until it's completely wet. Let it drip a minute or two so the excess water runs off.

2 Cover the work area with newspaper and start dyeing. Fabric dye soaks into the fabric instead of sitting on top like paint. The diagram shows guidelines for painting the background of the pillow. Don't worry about being precise. You want some sky, green tree, grass, and a tree trunk. Use cotton swabs as disposable paint brushes and paper plates as disposable palettes. Put a bit of dye on a plate, dip the swab, and brush it on the fabric. Let the fabric dry. Keep in mind that the dye lightens dramatically when dry. You can re-wet the fabric and apply more dye if necessary.

3 While the fabric is drying, wet some ribbon and pool it on a paper plate. Dab it with dye. Experiment with different color combinations. Some of the most unlikely can become your favorites. Our favorite turned out to be purple dye on pale orange ribbon! "Who'd a thunk it?"

4 When everything is dry, remove the fabric from the stretcher bars and follow the manufacturer's directions for heat setting the color if required. We tested our samples and they were colorfast. Be sure to test yours if you plan to wash the item. If you plan to dry clean it, take some sample fabric and ribbon to the dry cleaner to test. Now we're ready to create our Monet!

Ribbon Embroidery

Supplies

Dyed linen fabric (see above)
Yarn: dark brown, medium brown
2mm silk ribbon: green
4mm silk ribbon: light green, medium green, olive green, dark red, pink, fuchsia, burgundy, yellow, pale blue, mauve
7mm silk ribbon: green, hand-dyed variegated shades of green, olive, hand-dyed variegated shades of purples, hand-dyed variegated shades of gray/green for iris leaves
10mm Cottonaire: assorted hand-dyed greens and yellows
10mm rayon: purple
Beads: assorted browns, dusky blues, mauves, yellows
Fiberfill to fill pillow
Cotton cord for piping

1 Following the painted background, couch dark brown yarn back and forth to form a meandering path.

2 Couch the medium brown yarn along the tree trunk and up into the leaf area.

3 Use the ruching stitch on the tree leaves with the assorted dyed green ribbons and fill in with 7mm green ribbon.

4 Stitch a beaded stone fence in the center, using brown, dusky blue, and mauve beads.

5 Upper left of the fence, create a bush using the running ribbon stitch with 10mm hand-dyed Cottonaire ribbon.

6 The hollyhock border above the fence is created with ruched 4mm ribbons in various shades of reds, pinks, burgundies, and greens.

7 Just to right of the hollyhocks is a bush of 7mm olive green lazy daisies.

8 Below the fence to the left of the path are lazy daisy tulips. Start with the stems, using 7mm green ribbon and the twisted stem stitch. Add 4mm lazy daisy tulips and flat lazy daisy leaves.

9 Below them, larger than life, are wonderful lush tulips created with 10mm ribbons, using the same stitches as above. They are surrounded by 2mm flat lazy daisy foliage.

10 Moving directly across the path, we have more 2mm flat lazy daisy foliage. Just to the right are clumps of yellow loop stitch blossoms with lazy daisy leaves.

11 Above them are luscious iris. Start with twisted stem stitch stems, using 7mm hand-dyed ribbons. Continue with the flat lazy daisy leaves and create the iris with hand-dyed variegated purples using the lazy daisy stitch.

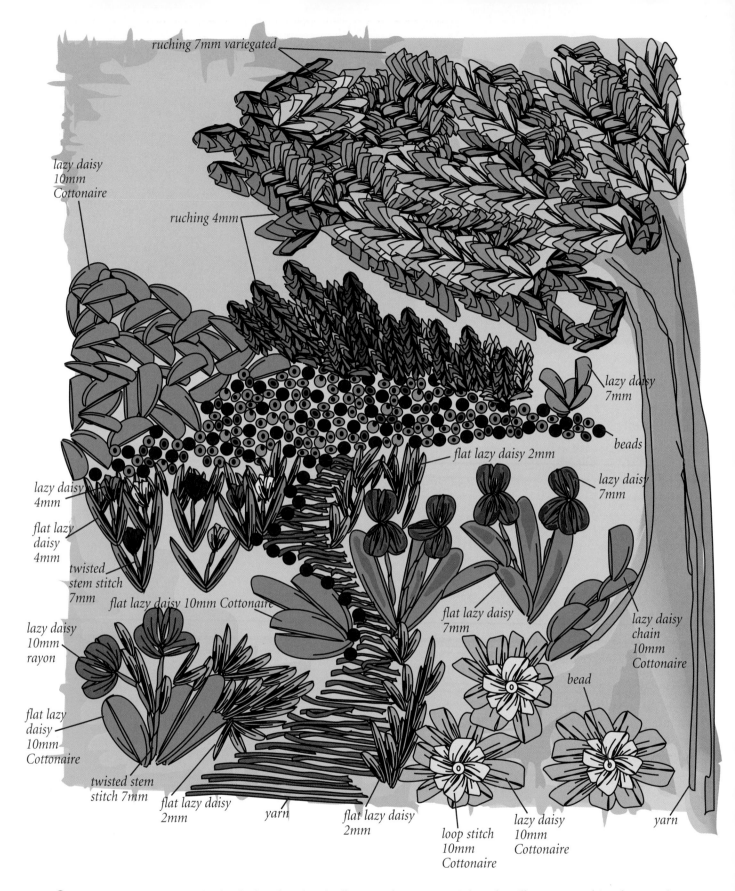

ruching 7mm variegated

lazy daisy 10mm Cottonaire

ruching 4mm

lazy daisy 7mm

beads

flat lazy daisy 2mm

lazy daisy 7mm

lazy daisy 4mm

flat lazy daisy 4mm

twisted stem stitch 7mm

flat lazy daisy 10mm Cottonaire

flat lazy daisy 7mm

lazy daisy chain 10mm Cottonaire

lazy daisy 10mm rayon

flat lazy daisy 10mm Cottonaire

bead

twisted stem stitch 7mm

flat lazy daisy 2mm

yarn

flat lazy daisy 2mm

loop stitch 10mm Cottonaire

lazy daisy 10mm Cottonaire

yarn

⑫ To finish the pillow, cut the finished embroidered pillow front 1″ beyond the design. Our finished design measured 10″ x 12″. We added 1″ on all sides and cut it 12″ x 14″. Follow the design for the exact measurements. Cut a back the same size.

⑬ Using leftover linen, make piping by covering cording with bias strips. Stitch to the pillow top, matching the raw edges.

⑭ With right sides together, stitch 1/2″ seam allowances, leaving a 4″ opening to turn.

⑮ Clip the corners, turn, and fill with fiberfill. Hand sew the opening closed.

*S*ummer weddings bring visions of shady glens with everyone dressed in their Sunday best, milling around conversing with friends and neighbors, trying to stay cool! Our straw hat was embellished with just that in mind. Choose a lightweight fabric such as chiffon and stitch on your favorite flowers. We roll hemmed the edges and tied it on our favorite straw hat.

Quick Project
Summer Hat

Supplies

Straw hat
1/2 yard chiffon, silk, or
   rayon
10mm Cottonaire
   ribbon: green, peach,
   purple
7mm ribbon: over-dyed
   green, white, pink
4mm ribbon: yellow,
   purple, green
Beads: yellow, avocado

❶ Cut the fabric in half into two 9″ x 45″ pieces. Seam them to form one long 9″ x 90″ piece. Stitch the ribbon embroidery over the center seam.

❷ Begin with 10mm chain stitch roses. Add lazy daisy leaves and lazy daisy flowers. Add the beads as you go. End with the ruching.

❸ To construct the finished hatband, turn the short ends under 1/4″ and again 1/4″. Stitch with a straight stitch.

❹ With right sides together, stitch the long seam, turn, and press. Tie to the hat and have a lovely time!

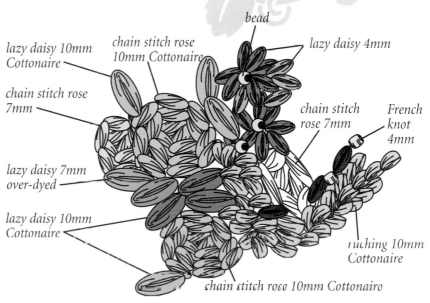

bead

lazy daisy 10mm Cottonaire

chain stitch rose 10mm Cottonaire

lazy daisy 4mm

chain stitch rose 7mm

chain stitch rose 7mm

French knot 4mm

lazy daisy 7mm over-dyed

lazy daisy 10mm Cottonaire

ruching 10mm Cottonaire

chain stitch rose 10mm Cottonaire

Chapter 6

Autumn Projects

Fall Flowers Grapevine Wreath

*F*or our autumn wreath, think of all the smells, sights, and sounds of the fall season! It's back to school—crisp clear days with deep blue skies, showing off nature's most colorful display of the year. The bright oranges and yellows, mixed with muted browns and purples on the quickly changing leaves. Late-blooming flowers which doggedly hang on 'til the first hard frost bring muted rusts, plums, and golden hues into the picture. Those of us in the "autumn" of our lives remember these sights and sounds accompanied by the smell of burning leaves! Though only a memory for most of us, the smell is still real, if only in our mind.

Supplies

16″ square of natural color linen or linen-like fabric

Yarn: assorted 4-ply knitting yarn, macramé yarn, or cotton cords in muted browns

4mm ribbon: medium purple, dark purple, hand-dyed variegated purple, dark mauve, rust, mulberry, gold, dark orange, mauve/gold variegated, olive green

7mm ribbon: rusty red, salmon, olive green

10mm Cottonaire: yellow-green

Beads: champagne

Liquid fabric stiffener

❶ Draw a 6″ circle (or whatever size you prefer) on the fabric with an air-soluble marker or chalk. Choose several shades and thicknesses of muted brown yarns and cords and couch them over the circle, creating a wreath about 1″-wide. Intertwine them as you go, pulling them under the previous strands with tweezers. Try stitching several strands down at once, twisting them as you go.

❷ Let's begin our decorations with the mums. Draw a 1″ circle and use 4mm dark mauve, rust, mulberry, and gold ribbons to make a ring around the perimeter with lazy daisy stitches. Fill the center with loop stitches of the same colors. Work with several colors at once: stitch several lazy daisies of one color, bring in another and do several more lazy daisies, then return to the original. Alternate two or three colors until done.

❸ Fill in between the mums with lazy daisy leaves of 4mm olive green.

❹ Nestle the pumpkin on the bottom of the wreath. Draw a pumpkin shape and divide it into four columns. Use 4mm dark orange ribbon to fill the columns with the fern stitch. Find a snippet of 4mm olive green and couch a stem.

❺ Stitch a stem for the columbines with 7mm olive green ribbon. Try the new twisted stitch. Sew the flowers with 4mm mauve/gold ribbon using the ruching stitch.

❻ The lush zinnias are made with 7mm rusty red ribbon, using lazy daisy stitches. Fill the centers with champagne colored beads. Embellish with yellow/green Cottonaire leaves, using the lazy daisy stitch.

❼ Satisfy your craving for purple by stitching a lush branch of lavender using 4mm medium, dark, and hand-dyed variegated purples. Use the ruching stitch.

❽ To make the curly tendrils, wrap some brown yarn around a large knitting needle or wooden dowel. Stiffen with fabric stiffener and let dry. Remove and cut into 1″ sections. Pull apart slightly and tack in place.

❾ The wreath can be mounted on stretcher bars and framed (as ours was) or made into a pillow or wall hanging. Keep in mind that the curly tendrils can't be washed or dry cleaned, so leave them off a project that will require cleaning.

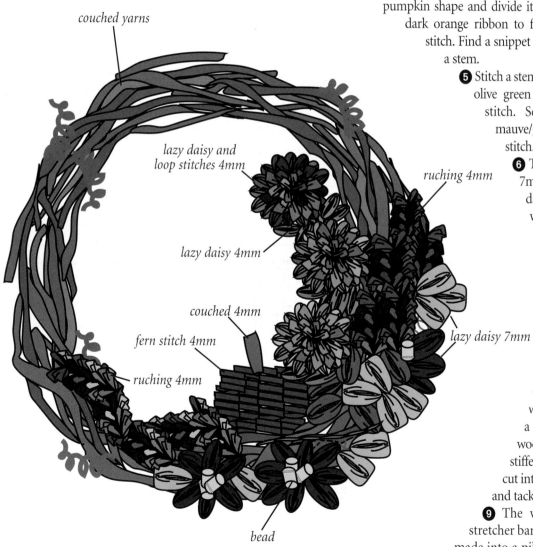

couched yarns

lazy daisy and loop stitches 4mm

lazy daisy 4mm

couched 4mm

fern stitch 4mm

ruching 4mm

ruching 4mm

lazy daisy 7mm

bead

Here are three fall designs for you to stitch for gift giving or to spruce up last year's fall outfit. The first design, Halloween Buddies, is for the ghoul lovers in your life.

The second, Cornucopia, incorporates a cornucopia button filled with a profusion of fall's bounty—a pumpkin, a mum, and some autumn foliage.

The third, Autumn Favorites, is a grouping of branches, a pumpkin, a flower, and some French knot berries.

Try any or all of these or choose your favorite designs from other projects. These are a great way to use the little samples that tend to collect when you practice a technique or flower before stitching it on the project.

Quick Project
Covered Button Pins

Supplies

1⅞″ to 2″ diameter covered button kits

Scraps of dark brown and black velvet, wool, felt, or Ultrasuede

1 cornucopia button by Blumenthal

4mm ribbon: burgundy, white, plum, purple, rust, rust/green hand-dyed variegated, dark brown

7mm ribbon: dark red, rust/plum hand-dyed variegated

Beads: black

Pin backs

Permanent fabric glue (such as Aleene's OK to Wash It glue)

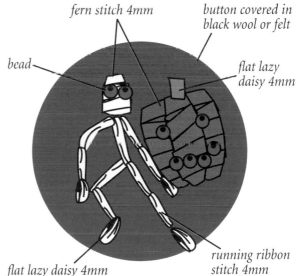

fern stitch 4mm

button covered in black wool or felt

bead

flat lazy daisy 4mm

flat lazy daisy 4mm

running ribbon stitch 4mm

Halloween Buddies

❶ Our skeleton friend is a combination of stitches. Start by tracing around the covered button form and sketching his "stick" figure with chalk.

❷ Use 4mm white ribbon with the fern stitch to create his head. Begin sewing the ribbon at the top of his head.

❸ Without cutting the ribbon, continue with the running ribbon stitch to create his trunk and one leg. Finish his foot, with a flat lazy daisy stitch, tuck the end under, and tack in place.

4 Start the ribbon over at his waist and repeat for his other leg.

5 For his arms and hands, start with a lazy daisy stitch for a hand, continue with a running ribbon stitch arm, right on over his shoulder and down his other arm. Finish with a lazy daisy hand.

6 The pumpkin's easy! Do three rows of fern stitches using 4mm rust ribbon. Top with a flat lazy daisy stitch, 4mm dark brown stem.

7 Give both the skeleton and the pumpkin eyes and mouths with beads and say, "Look out, here we come!"

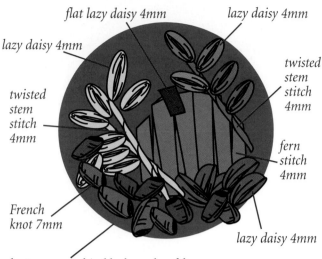

flat lazy daisy 4mm

lazy daisy 4mm

lazy daisy 4mm

twisted stem stitch 4mm

twisted stem stitch 4mm

fern stitch 4mm

French knot 7mm

lazy daisy 4mm

button covered in black wool or felt

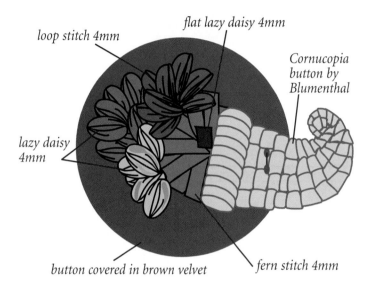

loop stitch 4mm

flat lazy daisy 4mm

Cornucopia button by Blumenthal

lazy daisy 4mm

button covered in brown velvet

fern stitch 4mm

Cornucopia

1 Trace the circle shape of the button on the fabric with chalk. The cornucopia button will extend off the edge of the fabric. Following the circle guidelines, stitch the button in place or trace its shape so the stitching holding the button on is at the edge of the covered button circle. Now you know where to place the ribbon embroidery.

2 Use 4mm rust ribbon to make a "punkin," half in and half out of the cornucopia button. Stitch this by starting in the center where the stem is and fanning the ribbon stitches out, pivoting from this center point.

3 Use 4mm dark brown to add a flat lazy daisy stem.

4 Stitch the mum with the loop stitch and 4mm purple ribbon.

5 Below the mum, add an autumn bloom using 4mm variegated rust/green hand-dyed ribbon. We used the lazy daisy stitch.

6 Finish with the lazy daisy stitch and 4mm burgundy ribbon to create a blossom that peeks out from behind other flowers.

Autumn Favorites

1 Trace the circle shape of the button on the fabric with chalk, leaving enough around the perimeter to hoop the

fabric. Keep the embroidery within the button circle. Sketch a 1″ circle in the shape of a pumpkin.

2 Use 4mm rust ribbon to create a pumpkin with the fern stitch. Add a 4mm dark brown stem with a flat lazy daisy stitch.

3 Next we'll stitch the branches to overlap the pumpkin. Start with 4mm cream colored ribbon and sew a stem using the twisted stem stitch. Add some lazy daisy leaves as shown. Repeat with 4mm rust/green hand-dyed variegated ribbon and create the other branch.

4 Stitch some French knot berries around the bottom curve, using 7mm dark red and rust/plum hand-dyed variegated ribbons.

5 Complete the design with a lazy daisy flower, using 4mm plum with a 7mm dark red French knot center.

Finish the Pins

Finishing the button pins is easiest if you use the following directions instead of those on the package. This is because our fabrics tend to be too heavy for the package directions.

1 Cut out the circle, adding 1/2″ beyond the line you've drawn indicating the button size. Double thread a hand needle and do a running stitch around the edge of the circle. Place the fabric on the button form and pull up the hand sewn stitches, securing the fabric around the button form. Take a few stitches to secure the threads and set aside.

2 Remove the metal sew-on loop with a pair of pliers. Cut a fabric circle from wool or felt the size of the back. Use the zigzag stitch on the sewing machine or hand stitch the pin in place on the fabric circle.

3 Glue the metal back in place and let it dry. Glue the fabric circle with the pin sewn on it over the metal backing.

Falling Leaves Vest

Our vest was inspired by the magnificent color display that Mother Nature puts on in October each year. Smell the aroma of burning leaves, picture the kids raking the leaves, only to roll around in them and then come in the house to warm up with hot chocolate! The colors are unique—the bright oranges and yellows of the maples, the wonderful plums and deep, deep purples. We found the perfect fabric—an all-over print with leaves. The background is cream and the leaves are a perfect size, about 3″ to 4″. Although you may not find our exact print, you will find one similar.

Supplies

Basic vest pattern (no darts)
1½ yards dark brown 100% cotton fabric
1/2 yard leaf motif fabric
1 yard double-sided iron-on stabilizer (Wonder Under™)
Dark brown sewing thread
4mm ribbon: assorted brown, gold, plum, orange to coordinate with fabric
7mm ribbon: assorted brown, gold, plum, orange to coordinate with fabric
1 pkg. water-soluble stabilizer such as Solvy™ by Sulky
Beads: large round brown for acorns

① Both the lining and the vest are cut from dark brown cotton. Make one dark brown outer vest. This is where you'll apply the leaf motif fabric to the front. Make a second dark brown vest as a lining. If the pattern has facings, don't use them. The pattern doesn't need to have lining pattern pieces because you'll use the same outer pattern pieces for both the vest and lining.

cut edge of fabric

base fabric

individually cut out motifs

② Cut four vest fronts and two vest backs from dark brown cotton. Set aside all but two of the vest fronts.

③ Apply Wonder Under to the back of the leaf motif fabric according to the manufacturer's directions. Remove the paper backing.

④ Lay the two vest fronts on the leaf motif fabric as shown and cut around the vest shape.

⑤ Remove the brown cotton vest bases. Cut around the leaf shapes across the bottom.

⑥ Place the leaf motif pieces on the brown and look at them. We trimmed out some of the background fabric between a few leaves here and there near the bottom.

⑦ Cut out a few leaves from the extra fabric to scatter across the bottom.

⑧ When satisfied with the design, iron the leaf motifs in place according to the manufacturer's directions.

⑨ Set your sewing machine for ribbon embroidery, following the instructions on page 9. Embellish a few leaves on the upper section of the vest and cover the raw edges of the cut leaves across the bottom. Use appropriate colors of 4mm and 7mm ribbons. You may want to try the running ribbon stitch, the chained knot stitch, and couching-with-a-twist. As you are doing the ribbon embroidery, add a few bead acorns.

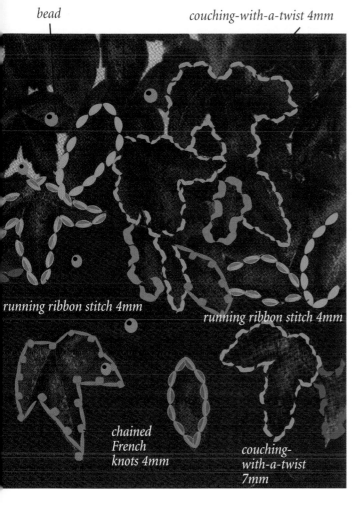

bead   couching-with-a-twist 4mm

running ribbon stitch 4mm   running ribbon stitch 4mm

chained French knots 4mm

couching-with-a-twist 7mm

⓮ Set the machine for regular sewing. Sew the shoulder seams in the vest. Press open the seams.

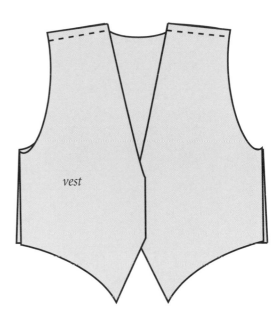

vest

⓮ Sew the shoulder seams in the vest lining. Press open the seams.

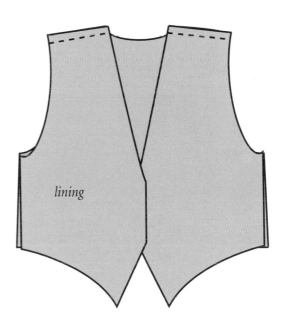

lining

⓾ Lay some extra cutout leaves wrong sides together on scraps of dark brown cotton. Fuse them according to the manufacturer's directions. Cut out the leaves. Place the Solvy in a hoop and lay a fused leaf on top of the Solvy. Anchor the leaf to the Solvy by stitching near the edge.

⓫ Do one of the above ribbon embroidery stitches around the edge. Repeat for as many leaves as will fit in the hoop. Remove from the hoop and trim away the excess Solvy.

⓬ Place a few leaves on the vest and tack in place. Save some to make our Quick Project Napkin Rings.

⓯ Place the vest and the lining right sides together and begin stitching on the bottom front, a few inches from the side seam. Stitch across the bottom, up the center front, around the neck, back down the front, and across the other bottom, stopping several inches short of the side seam. Stitch the armholes. Trim and clip all the curves. Hint: Use pinking shears to trim and you won't have to clip the curves.

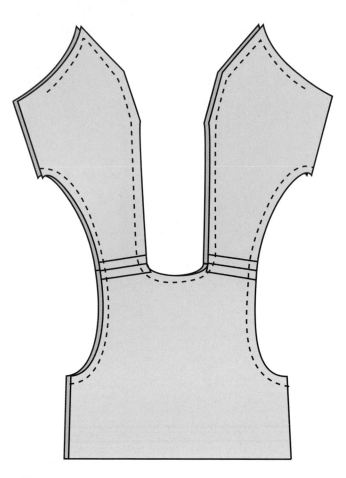

17 Place the vest side seams right sides together and pin, matching the armhole seams. Stitch, continuing onto the lining, completing the lining side seam. Repeat for the other set of side seams but leave a 4″ opening in the lining portion. Press.

16 Reach through the shoulder from the bottom back and turn right sides out. Press.

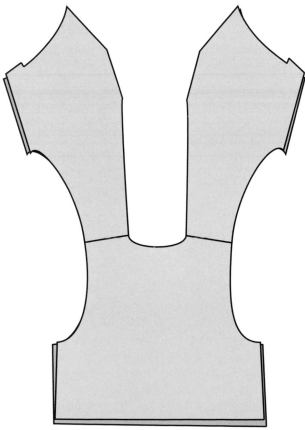

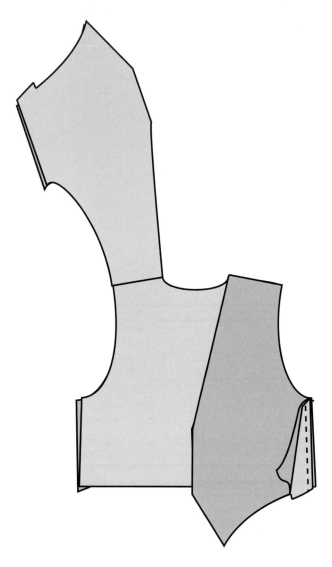

18 Reach in through the hole in the lining side seam and pull the bottom back of the vest out through the hole. Stitch with right sides together. Pull back through the hole and press. Hand stitch the 4″ opening in the lining.

Quick Project
Napkin Rings

A dd a touch of autumn color to the table with these leaf napkin rings. They would even dress up everyday paper napkins!

Supplies

Scraps of leaf motif fabric
Scraps of dark brown 100% cotton
Wonder Under fusible web
4mm ribbon: assorted to coordinate with leaf fabric
7mm ribbon: assorted to coordinate with leaf fabric
1 cut strip 2½″ x 6″ dark brown 100% cotton for each napkin ring
1 cut strip 2½″ x 6″ fleece for each napkin ring
Water-soluble stabilizer (such as Solvy)

❶ Apply Wonder Under to the back of the leaf motif fabric according to the manufacturer's directions.

❷ Fuse to scraps of dark brown cotton, following the manufacturer's directions. Cut out the leaves.

❸ Place Solvy in the hoop and set the machine for ribbon embroidery following the directions on page 9. Lay the cut leaf on the Solvy and baste it in place by stitching around the leaf near the edge.

❹ Stitch ribbon embroidery around the outer edge of the leaf, using the running ribbon stitch, the couching-with-a-twist stitch, or chained knots.

❺ Remove from the hoop and trim away the excess Solvy.

❻ Set the machine for regular stitching. Make the napkin rings by placing the dark brown strip on top of the fleece strip and stitching around the outer edge.

❼ Fold right sides together lengthwise and sew the long edge. Turn the resulting tube right side out. Hint: A Fast Turn Tube™ is wonderful for this.

❽ Place one or two embroidered leaves in the center of the tube and tack in place

❾ Fold right sides together and form a loop. Stitch and turn.

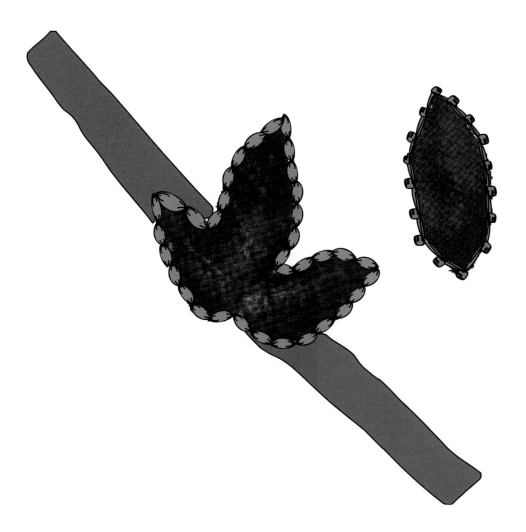

November

Fall Door Knob Decoration

Supplies

1/2 yard solid brown cotton or muted geometric print
1/2 yard coordinating plum or autumn colored cotton print for lining
4mm ribbon: hand-dyed variegated rust/green, plum, green
7mm ribbon: hand-dyed variegated plum/rust
10mm Cottonaire: hand-dyed plum, green
12″ square of Wonder Under fusible web
Pinking shears

*B*ring the spirit of autumn into the house with this door-knob decoration. It's actually a "lunch" bag with a handle. Fill it with dried flowers and hang it on the front door to welcome guests. Leave off the handle, add some potpourri and a bit of sand in the bottom for stability, and you have an instant centerpiece for the Thanksgiving table or an accent to celebrate the fall season on any occasional table in the house!

Cut:
12″ square brown fabric
12″ square of plum lining fabric
4″ x 4″ strip of either fabric for handle

1 Because you can't iron over ribbon embroidery, fuse the two layers together before starting. Place the Wonder Under with the "rough" glue side down, on the wrong side of the brown fabric. Iron for about ten seconds or until you can remove the paper backing. Pull off the paper. Place the brown fabric wrong sides together with the plum lining fabric and fuse. Follow the manufacturer's directions for the exact timing.

2 Find the center and measure up 2″ from the bottom. Mark with chalk or an air-soluble marker. This is the bottom of the ribbon embroidery. Draw a 1½″ square with chalk or an air-soluble marker on this mark. This is where you'll weave the basket.

3 Using the hand-dyed variegated rust/green ribbon, stitch the fern stitch to cover the marked square. Use tweezers to pull the ribbon where you want it and weave it back and forth through the fern stitch.

4 Now fill the basket with flowers! Start with 4mm plum and stitch a circle of lazy daisies and fill it in with loop stitches.

5 The lilies are running ribbon stitches of 7mm hand-dyed variegated rust/plum. Add stems using the twisted stem stitch in 4mm green. The leaves are sewn with 10mm Cottonaire using the running ribbon stitch.

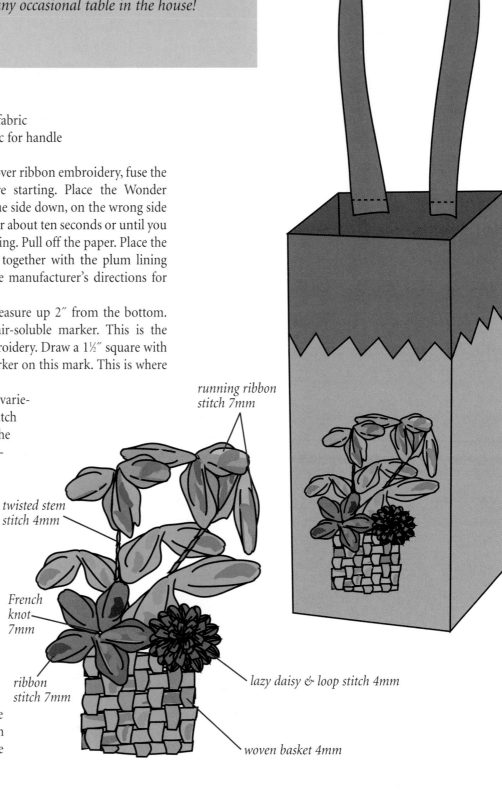

running ribbon stitch 7mm

twisted stem stitch 4mm

French knot 7mm

ribbon stitch 7mm

lazy daisy & loop stitch 4mm

woven basket 4mm

6 Add the fall flower with hand-dyed plum/green Cottonaire lazy daisy stitches. Fill the center with a 7mm plum/rust French knot.

7 To construct the bag, set the machine for regular straight stitch. Fold in half with right sides together and stitch the seam, top to bottom.

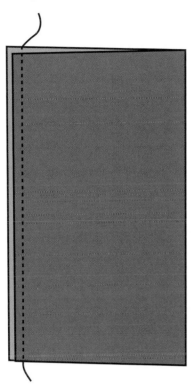

8 Fold so the seam is in the center and stitch across the bottom.

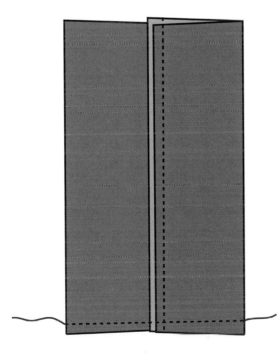

9 To form the bottom, bring the bottom seam to meet the side and measure up 1″. Sew across the resulting triangle as shown. Trim off the triangle and turn right side out.

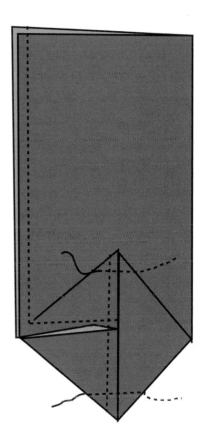

10 Trim the top edge with pinking shears and fold down about 2″.

11 To make the handles, fold the 4″ x 14″ piece of fabric in half lengthwise and press. Fold again lengthwise, making a piece 1″ x 14″. Press and stitch near the edge.

12 Mark 1″ on either side of the center back seam and use these marks to position the handles. Stitch the handles in place.

Quick Project
Miniature Purse Necklace

Supplies

Miniature purse top
Pleated silk fabric (or any lightweight soft fabric)
4mm silk ribbon: bright green, grayed green, brown, gold, over-dyed rust, over-dyed red/mauve
Beads: small purple iridescent
Matching chain for necklace

In times past, ladies sometimes wore miniature purses around their necks, both for decoration and for keeping a pill or a special treasure. These were a necessary piece of adornment and did serve a purpose. The ladies either wore them on a chain or a pretty ribbon to match the outfit of the day.

To make this miniature purse, we purchased a small purse top (the source is listed in the back).

You can find similar pieces in craft stores or order them through magazines. Follow the instructions that come with purse top telling how large to cut the fabric. Ours was 3″ x 8″. Read through all the instructions to find when to add the embellishment. Ours had the fabric on the purse top. Instead of sewing both sides, we sewed one, added the embellishment, and then completed according to their instructions.

fern stitch 4mm

loop stitch 4mm

loop stitch 4mm

lazy daisies filled with loop stitches 4mm

French knot 4mm

French knot 4mm

loop stitch 4mm

loop stitch 4mm

bead

carrying stitch 4mm

carrying stitch 4mm

❶ Assemble the purse according to the instructions, stopping to add embellishment before completing.

❷ We made French knots in a row with over-dyed rust ribbon and a couple looped leaves in green. Beside this is a small green fern stitched leaf.

❸ At the base of the fern is a loop stitched small mum done in rust and gold. Add an iridescent bead in the center.

❹ To the right of the fern is 4mm dark green ribbon anchored and topped with two loop stitches as buds. Carry the green down into a looped leaf and stem.

❺ This stem continues to make more stem and another leaf. We cut this green ribbon and continued on with a vertical loop stitched flower made with 4mm over-dyed red/mauve.

❻ The back side of the purse features a multi-colored chrysanthemum made with lazy daisy stitches and filled in the center with loop stitches. We used gold and over-dyed brown to complete this flower.

❼ Make a 4mm green stem and carry the stitch. Top with a bullion bud and a few petals for the mum that's about to open. Finish the green in a loop stitch leaf.

❽ Make a brown stem using a carrying stitch topped with small French knots and a couple small loops to finish the purse.

❾ Finish the lower end of the purse, again following the directions on the pattern and enjoy the compliments. The purse can hold a bus token, a few coins, or an aspirin to help soothe you on one of those hectic days!

Chapter 7

Winter Projects

December

Winter Grapevine Wreath

*F*or our Winter Wreath, we chose from seasonal greens fragrant with pungent evergreen woody smells, pine cones, berries that survive the harsh winter weather, and hothouse flowers coaxed out of their winter sleep to bring us color and life in the holiday season! The bright red poinsettias and the sprigs of white blossoms with their cheerful red centers add color to the deep greens and browns of the foliage.

Supplies

16″ square of natural color linen or linen-like fabric

Assorted yarn: 4-ply knitting yarn, macramé yarn, or cotton cords in muted browns, dark green boucle, dark green pearl rayon

2mm ribbon: forest green

4mm ribbon: white, brown

7mm ribbon: hand-dyed variegated blue/green, red

Beads: red, yellow, clear

Liquid fabric stiffener

1 Draw a 6″ circle (or whatever size you prefer) on the fabric with an air-soluble marker or chalk. Choose several shades and thicknesses of muted brown yarns and cords and couch them over the circle, creating a wreath about 1″-wide. Intertwine them as you go, pulling them under the previous strands with tweezers. Try stitching several strands down at once, twisting them as you go.

2 Begin with the poinsettias. Use 7mm red ribbon to make ribbon stitch petals radiating out from the center. Stitch three or four yellow and clear beads in each center.

3 Using 2mm forest green, stitch the stems and leaves for the sprig of white flowers. Sew the flowers with 4mm white ribbon and embellish the base of each with a red bead.

4 Use blue/green hand-dyed ribbon to create holly leaves using the ribbon stitch. A red bead here and there completes the look of holly berries.

5 The pine cones nestle among the evergreens and are sewn with the fern stitch, using 4mm brown ribbon. Start with a row of fern stitches at the top of the pine cone and continue to stitch three or four rows down.

6 Finish by filling in the gaps with evergreen boughs, using dark green boucle yarn and dark green pearl rayon. Simply sew long, flat lazy daisies.

7 Add clusters of red berries for a bright spot of color among the dark green boughs.

8 To make the curly tendrils, wrap some brown yarn around a large knitting needle or wooden dowel. Stiffen with fabric stiffener and let dry. Remove and cut into 1″ sections. Pull apart slightly and tack in place.

9 The wreath can be mounted on stretcher bars and framed (as ours was) or made into a pillow or wall hanging. Keep in mind that the curly tendrils can't be washed or dry cleaned, so leave them off a project that will require cleaning.

couched boucle yarn

couched yarns

lazy daisy 4mm

lazy daisy 2mm

fern stitch 4mm

ribbon stitch 7mm

ribbon stitch 7mm

couched boucle yarn

bead

Father Christmas

*F*ather Christmas can run the gamut from a country cousin with straw for his beard and a burlap bag to our Father Christmas, also known as Santa, St. Nicholas, and many other variations. Ours is so elegant, he couldn't possibly be anything but "Father."

We chose the richest of velvets, the showiest beads, the most sparkly metallic cords and ribbons, and the satiniest of cords. Only the best for Father. Please don't tell anyone his body is a recycled pop bottle. He would truly be offended!

Supplies

Santa head with beard and mustache (Ours was an ornament purchased at Marshall Fields. If you have trouble finding one, try craft stores or catalogs. Ours is about 3″ in diameter. We made him a new hat.)

1 yard green crushed velvet

1/2 yard green satin

1/2 yard silver crushed velvet

1/2 yard green 1/4″ satin twisted cording for cape string closure

2mm ribbon: green, raspberry

4mm ribbon: mauve

7mm ribbon: cranberry

2mm metallic cord: green, cranberry

Green boucle cord

Beads: bright pink, mauve, purple

1 yard green rat tail satin cord for bag drawstring

12″ cord for drawstring on robe

Regular sewing thread: green, pale gray

Fiberfill

Hot glue gun or white craft glue

2 liter plastic soda bottle for body

2 lb. rice or other material to weight the body

Optional depending on the head size: 2″ to 4″ round wooden base and matching green paint

Cut:

Green crushed velvet:

12″ x 18″ for robe

12″ x 16″ for cape

12″ x 12″ for hat (cutting instructions follow)

(2) 3″ x 12″ strips for sleeves

Green satin:

2″ x 16″ for cape

Silver crushed velvet:

(2) 6″ x 12″ for embroidered cape panels

3″ x 12″ for embroidered hatband

(4) mittens from pattern

Optional:

6″ x 16″ for bottom cape band

(2) 8″ x 4½″ for bag

❶ Prepare the head as necessary. Remove the hat, if applicable. Expose the neck, removing any stuffing (if applicable) so it can be glued on the bottle.

❷ Wash and thoroughly dry an empty two liter soda bottle. Fill it about halfway with rice, kitty litter, or sand to weight it. Glue the head in place, using either a hot glue gun or white craft glue.

❸ Fold one 6″ x 12″ cape panel in half with right sides together. Stitch the two short ends. Repeat for the other panel. Turn right side out and set aside for embroidery.

❹ Prepare the 3″ x 12″ hatband by folding it wrong sides together. Set aside for embroidery.

❺ Set the machine for ribbon embroidery, following the directions on page 9. Refer to the diagram to complete the ribbon embroidery. On the cape panel, be sure to leave 1″ of fabric unembroidered from the raw edge to the seam of the finished cape. For the hat, center the embroidery on the prepared band. For the bag, center the embroidery on one of the 8″ x 4½″ bag pieces.

❻ Make the robe by hemming one 18″ edge of robe fabric. You can use a decorative thread in the serger as we did, or turn it up 1/4″ and straight stitch in place.

❼ Fold the other 18″ edge under 1/2″ and stitch a casing.

❽ Stitch the center back seam with right sides together, starting at the bottom and ending just before the casing. Insert the 12″ drawstring cord in the casing.

❾ Put the robe on the Santa, draw up the cord tightly, and knot.

❿ Mark and stitch three evenly spaced darts in the 12″ x 16″ velvet and satin pieces as shown.

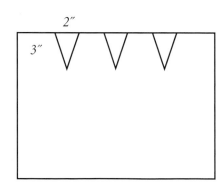

robe front design

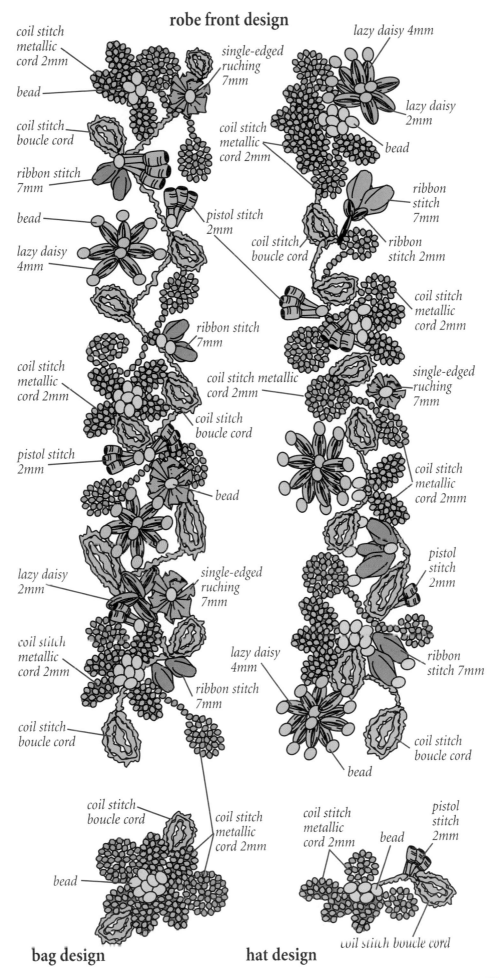

coil stitch
metallic
cord 2mm

bead

coil stitch
boucle cord

ribbon stitch
7mm

bead

lazy daisy
4mm

coil stitch
metallic
cord 2mm

pistol stitch
2mm

lazy daisy
2mm

coil stitch
metallic
cord 2mm

coil stitch
boucle cord

single-edged
ruching
7mm

coil stitch
metallic
cord 2mm

pistol stitch
2mm

ribbon stitch
7mm

coil stitch metallic
cord 2mm

coil stitch
boucle cord

bead

single-edged
ruching
7mm

ribbon stitch
7mm

lazy daisy 4mm

lazy daisy
2mm

bead

ribbon
stitch
7mm

ribbon
stitch 2mm

coil stitch
boucle cord

coil stitch
metallic
cord 2mm

single-edged
ruching
7mm

coil stitch
metallic
cord 2mm

pistol
stitch
2mm

ribbon
stitch 7mm

lazy daisy
4mm

coil stitch
boucle cord

bead

bag design

coil stitch
boucle cord

coil stitch
metallic
cord 2mm

bead

hat design

coil stitch
metallic
cord 2mm

bead

pistol
stitch
2mm

coil stitch boucle cord

⑪ Construct the cape by placing the 12″ x 16″ velvet and the 12″ x 16″ satin right sides together. Stitch the two short sides and one long side (without darts). Turn right side out and press carefully.

⑫ Cut the 1/4″ twisted cord in half. Turn the raw edges to the inside and hand or machine stitch the top together, catching the cord in the front corners as you sew.

⑬ Finish the cape by stitching the front embroidered panels in place. To do this, place the embroidered side of the panel to the lining of the cape. Stitch, catching only the outer embroidered piece. Turn the other edge under and hand stitch in place. Fold towards the cape and tack in place.

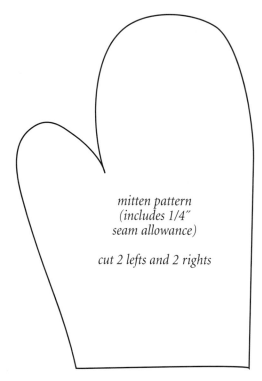

mitten pattern
(includes 1/4″
seam allowance)

cut 2 lefts and 2 rights

⑭ Place the mitten pieces right sides together and stitch, starting above the thumb and stitching halfway around. Attach the mittens to the sleeves with right sides together, then sew a mitten to the 3″ side of each sleeve piece.

⑮ With right sides together, continue around the mitten where you left off stitching and continue up the sleeve. Turn and lightly stuff the mittens (1/2 handful each).
Hint: Fast Turn Tubes are a wonderful tool to use to turn the sleeve/hands. Machine or hand stitch the mittens together, end to end. Machine or hand stitch the arms together at the other end, forming a circle. Place on Santa and tack in place at the back of his neck.

⑯ Put the cape on Santa. Depending on the size of his head, you may want to add an optional base. If you feel he needs a bit more height, add a circular wooden base (available at craft stores) and paint it green to match his outfit. Glue Santa in place with a glue gun or white craft glue. If you added the base, you'll need to add the optional band to the bottom of his cape. Fold right sides together and stitch the two short ends. Turn, press, and stitch to the bottom of his cape as you did the front panels.

⑰ Measure the circumference of Santa's head where his hat will sit. Add 1″ for ease and seam allowances. This will be the bottom of the triangle cut for his hat. Cut according to the illustration. Fold right sides together and stitch the diagonal edges. Place the embroidered band with the right side of the band on the wrong side of the hat and stitch. Join the band edges by hand to form a circle. Place a handful of fiberfill inside, put on Santa, and glue in place.

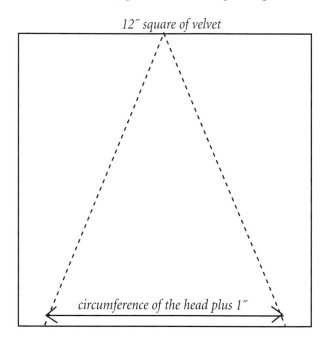

12″ square of velvet

circumference of the head plus 1″

⑱ Make the bag by placing two 8″ x 4½″ pieces right sides together. Stitch one long side. Turn the top edge under 1/2″ to form a casing. With right sides together, stitch the bottom and the other long edge, stopping just short of the casing opening. Refer to the directions for the Fall Doorknob Decoration on page 63 to square off the bottom. Fill with a handful of fiberfill and insert the drawstring.

⑲ Embellish Father Christmas as desired with greenery, presents, or any finery you find appropriate.

Quilted Velvet
Tree Skirt

*M*any families have a small tabletop tree in addition to, or instead of a big tree. We sized our tree skirt for a smaller tree (32″ across) but requirements for a larger version (42″ across) are given in parenthesis. Make the pyramid velvet ornaments on page 78 with the leftovers. Merry Christmas!

Sew the Tree Skirt

1 Make the tree skirt before adding the ribbon embroidery. Cut the velvet into two circles, 34″ (44″) across. To cut circles, fold the velvet in half and in half again. Measure from the corner, 17″ (22″) out, pivoting from the corner out as shown.

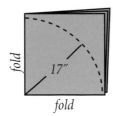

fold

fold

17″

2 Cut from the outer edge to the center.

3 Place the two circles right sides together, matching the raw edges, and lay them on top of the batting squares.

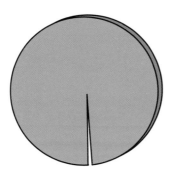

4 Stitch all the way around with a 1/4″ seam allowance, leaving an 8″ opening. Trim the excess batting, clip the corners, and turn.

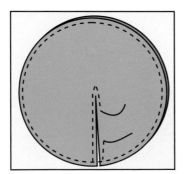

5 Press carefully, being careful not to crush the velveteen fibers. Hold the iron above the fabric, just barely touching it and steam. Hand stitch the hole closed.

Supplies

2 yards green cotton velveteen or velvet (3 yards)
34″ square of batting or fleece (44″)
Even feed or dual feed foot for sewing machine
4mm twin needle
2 spools red sewing thread
Yarn: medium green
Boucle cord: dark green
DMC rayon floss: bright green
7mm ribbon: red, green, pale greenish white, white, dark red
4mm ribbon: red, green, white,
Beads: green and white Fimo, green, red, white, dark red, yellow, chartreuse

6 Use a yardstick to mark off the beginning quilting lines with a chalk pencil or air-soluble marker.

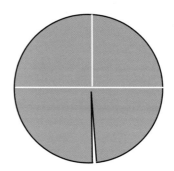

7 **Twin needle quilting**: There are a variety of twin needles available for sewing machines. Most sewing machines can accommodate a twin needle. The ones that can't are straight stitch only machines and ones that load the bobbin from the side. If you can't use a twin needle, you can still quilt with a single row of stitching. The twin needle for this project can be 2mm to 4mm. This measurement refers to the distance between the two needles. A twin needle has one shank with two needles coming down from it.

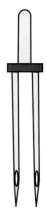

⑧ Baste the tree skirt by hand, taking large stitches or pinning with safety pins. Lay it on a table so it's flat, and baste about 6″ to 8″ apart.

⑨ Set the machine for quilting by placing the even feed foot or dual feed foot (walking foot) on the machine. This prevents the multiple layers from shifting as you sew. Using the straight stitch, topstitch the outer edge using the edge of the foot as a guide. Place the quilting guide on the machine. This guide (shown below) comes with most machines or can be purchased as an accessory. It allows you to sew multiple lines without marking each one. If you don't have a quilting guide, you can mark the skirt with a 2″ grid.

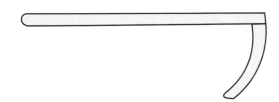

⑩ Thread the machine with two spools of red thread. Most machines have a metal dividing plate in the tension assembly to accommodate two threads. Place one thread to one side of this plate and the other thread on the other side. Thread one thread in each needle eye. There is only one bobbin. That's why the resulting stitch has straight stitches on the top of the work and the underside is a zigzag as shown. Sew with a straight stitch.

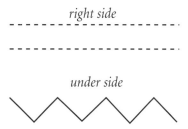

right side

under side

⑪ Begin stitching on the marked line. To stitch the second line, line up the quilting guide 2″ from the first row. Stitch, keeping the quilting guide even with the first row of stitching. Continue until the first half is complete. Turn the skirt around and complete the second half. Repeat for the lines going in the other direction.

Ribbon Embroidery

❶ Now that the tree skirt is sewn and quilted, let's embellish it! Set the machine for ribbon embroidery as shown on page 9. Following the diagram, stitch the greens, the couched yarn, the DMC floss, and the couched boucle cord.

❷ Refer to the diagram and complete the flowers, leaves, and beads.

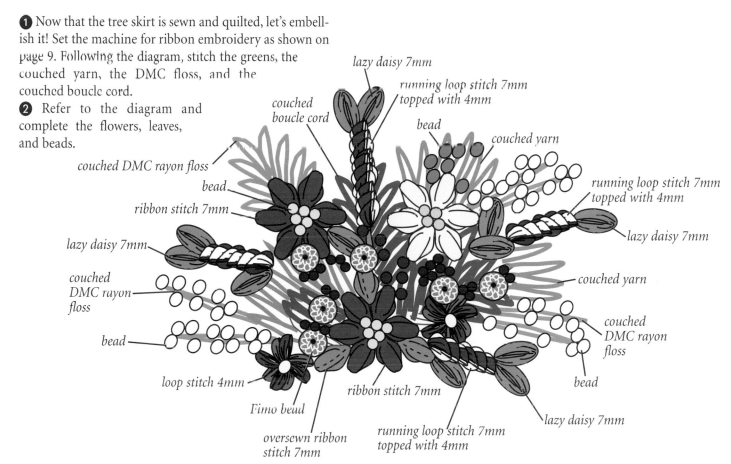

lazy daisy 7mm

running loop stitch 7mm topped with 4mm

couched boucle cord

bead

couched yarn

couched DMC rayon floss

bead

ribbon stitch 7mm

running loop stitch 7mm topped with 4mm

lazy daisy 7mm

couched yarn

lazy daisy 7mm

couched DMC rayon floss

bead

couched DMC rayon floss

bead

loop stitch 4mm

Fimo bead

oversewn ribbon stitch 7mm

ribbon stitch 7mm

running loop stitch 7mm topped with 4mm

lazy daisy 7mm

Pyramid Velvet Ornaments

Collect your "stash" of Christmas reds and greens...anything, as long as it's red and green. Cords, yarns, beads, ribbons, fabrics! We were into velveteen this year so we had scraps and a couple of remnants. That's where we started.

Then we wanted a shape. Square? No. Circle? No. What's left? A triangle? Okay, but give it dimension and it becomes a pyramid. Yessss! We purchased 25mm red/green ribbon by the yard at a fabric store. The same applies to the 13mm and 40mm sheer organza ribbon.

Supplies

2mm ribbon floss: green
DMC rayon floss: green
Yarn: green
2mm metallic cord: red
13mm and 40mm sheer organza ribbon: see samples for colors
25mm silk ribbon: red/green
4mm ribbon: red, white, green
7mm ribbon: green, red, white,
Beads: assorted red, green, and yellow beads, green and white Fimo beads
Fiberfill stuffing
12″ piece of 3/8″-wide satin ribbon for hanging loop for each ornament

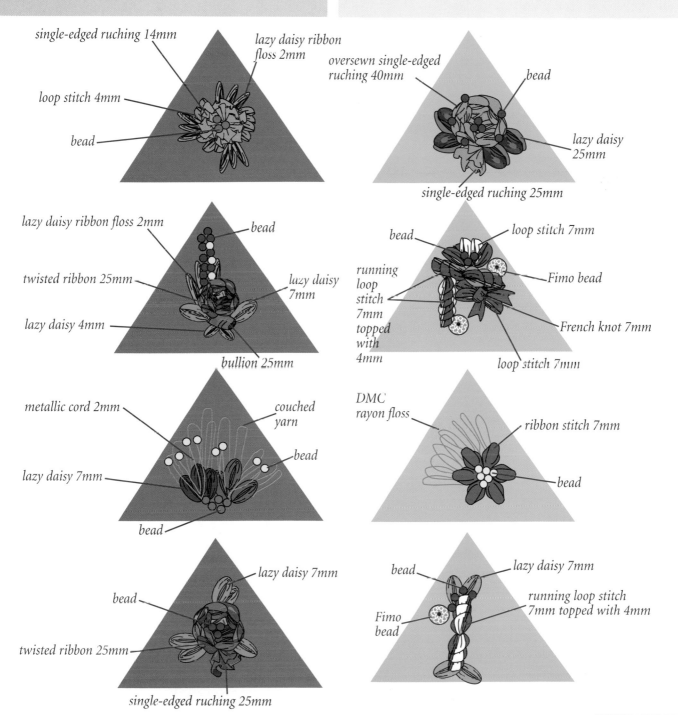

single-edged ruching 14mm
lazy daisy ribbon floss 2mm
loop stitch 4mm
bead

oversewn single-edged ruching 40mm
bead
lazy daisy 25mm
single-edged ruching 25mm

lazy daisy ribbon floss 2mm
bead
twisted ribbon 25mm
lazy daisy 7mm
lazy daisy 4mm
bullion 25mm

bead
loop stitch 7mm
running loop stitch 7mm topped with 4mm
Fimo bead
French knot 7mm
loop stitch 7mm

metallic cord 2mm
couched yarn
bead
lazy daisy 7mm
bead

DMC rayon floss
ribbon stitch 7mm
bead

lazy daisy 7mm
bead
twisted ribbon 25mm
single-edged ruching 25mm

bead
lazy daisy 7mm
running loop stitch 7mm topped with 4mm
Fimo bead

1 Mark off the triangle shape on the fabric with chalk and stitch the ribbon embroidery designs according to the diagrams. The running loop stitch topped with a second color is shown on page 18. Because we wanted our Fimo beads to sit with the hole up so the design would show, we took one stitch to the left of the bead, one stitch in the center hole, and then one stitch to the right of the bead.

2 Now assemble the pyramids. Our example uses red for the embroidered section and green for the sides. Use the triangle pattern below and cut out the embroidered design. Cut three more triangles from the same pattern.

3 Sew one green triangle to the embroidered red triangle and open out.

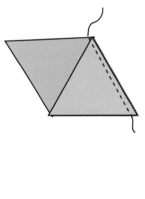

4 Sew another green triangle to the red triangle and open out

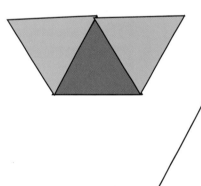

5 Sew the third green triangle to the red triangle and open out.

6 Finish by sewing A to A, leaving a 2″ opening to turn, B to B, and C to C. Turn and lightly stuff. Hand sew the openings shut.

7 Form a loop and bow from the 12″ piece of satin ribbon and hand or machine stitch to the top of the pyramid.

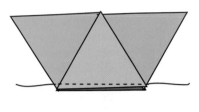

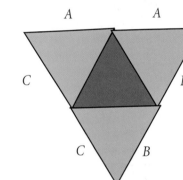

actual size pattern

5½″

Log Cabin Christmas Ornaments

Supplies

Assorted jewel tone velveteen or fabrics of your
    choice, cut into 1¼″ strips
Plum velveteen or your choice, large enough to fit
    in the hoop (for center embroidery)
4mm ribbon: bright green, bright blue, navy blue,
    plum (or colors to coordinate with the fabrics)
Beads: pink, blue
Regular sewing thread
Purchased 3″ tassel
Handful of fiberfill for each ornament

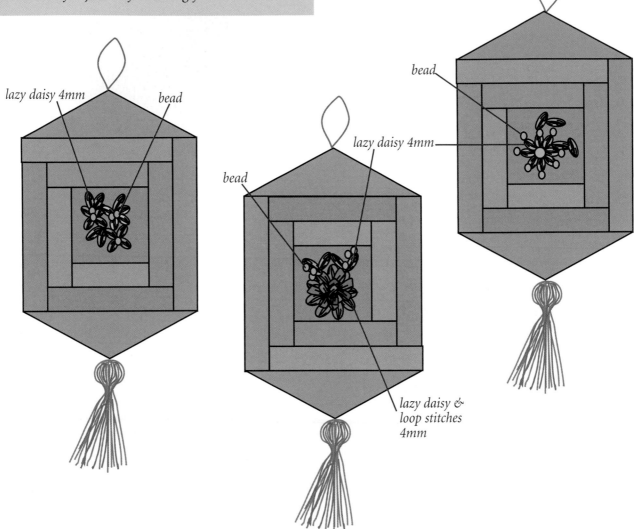

*W*e used scraps of velveteen left from other projects for our Log Cabin Christmas Ornaments. If you have other fabrics you would like to use, choose solids or monotone prints so as not to distract from the ribbon embroidery. These are a great way to try out stitches and flowers and create a wonderful decoration for yourself or as a gift.

lazy daisy 4mm

bead

bead

lazy daisy 4mm

bead

lazy daisy 4mm

lazy daisy & loop stitches 4mm

❶ Begin by setting the machine for ribbon embroidery, following the instructions on page 9.

❷ Refer to the diagrams above or choose your favorite flowers to embroider. Keep the embroidery less than 1½″ across.

❸ Trim the embroidered square to 2¼″ square.

❹ Choose a strip and place it right side down on the embroidered square. Stitch as shown, then trim the excess from the end of the strip and open out.

5 Place the next strip as shown and sew. Trim the excess from the end of the strip and open out.

6 Repeat with the next strip.

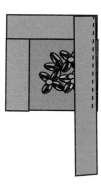

7 Repeat again with the next strip.

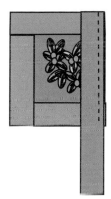

8 You now have four strips in place. You can quit if you like or do one more round as we did. Repeat the above directions until you have one more strip on each side.

9 Press the finished patchwork square, being careful not to flatten the ribbon embroidery. Measure one side. Draw a triangle on a scrap of velvet using this measurement as the long side and measuring up about 2″. Cut two of these triangles for each ornament.

10 With right sides together, stitch the triangles on top and bottom as shown. Press.

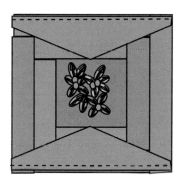

11 With right sides together, pin the patchwork on top of a piece of velvet. Don't try to cut it to size now, sew it first, and then trim it. That way if it shifts a bit, you won't be in trouble.

12 Pull out a strand of the tassel to use as the hanging loop. Insert the hanging loop and the tassel between the two layers.

13 Stitch around the outside, using a 1/4″ seam allowance. Leave a 2″ opening to turn it on a straight side. An even feed or walking foot for the sewing machine will make the velveteen layers feed through more easily.

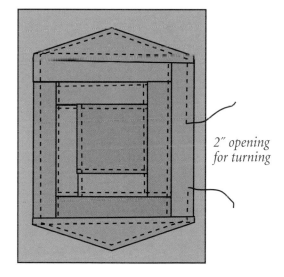

2″ opening for turning

14 Trim off the excess fabric and turn. Stuff lightly with fiberfill and hand stitch the opening closed.

Supplies

Fabric scraps for stocking and lining
7mm ribbon: red, pale green, white
Beads: yellow

Stocking Ornaments

*S*titch up several stocking ornaments as holders for checks or money or as a special gift for teachers, friends, or acquaintances. We chose velveteen, but any cotton, satin, or other scraps of beautiful fabric would be suitable.

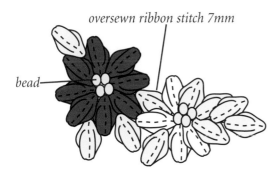

oversewn ribbon stitch 7mm

bead

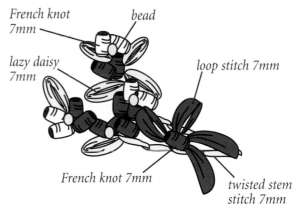

French knot 7mm

bead

lazy daisy 7mm

loop stitch 7mm

French knot 7mm

twisted stem stitch 7mm

❶ Trace the stocking pattern on paper and cut it out. Trace the stocking shape on the fabric but don't cut it out yet. You need a large enough piece of fabric to hoop.

❷ Place the fabric in the hoop and stitch the ribbon embroidery following the diagrams. Stitch the poinsettias first and then the leaves. Bead the centers when you are finished with the flowers. Follow the beading directions on page 20.

❸ On the second stocking, make the Christmas buds with the twisted stem stitch first, since it's behind the flowers. Stitch the French knot buds, adding the beads as you go. Fill in some lazy daisy leaves and finish with a loop stitch bow with a French knot center.

❹ Remove the fabric from the hoop and cut around the stocking shape, adding 1/4″ seam allowance.

❺ Using this as a pattern, cut out another outer stocking and two linings. (Be careful that you have the right and wrong sides of the fabric so you don't end up with one right and one left stocking.)

❻ Place the outer stockings right sides together, pin and stitch around the outer edge. Repeat with the lining, leaving a 3″ opening in the side for turning.

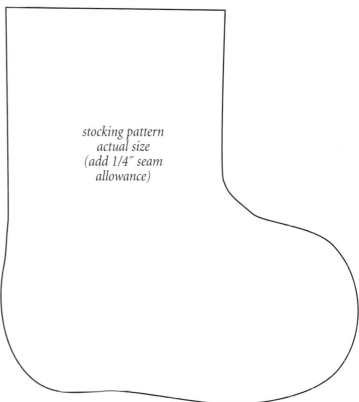

stocking pattern actual size (add 1/4″ seam allowance)

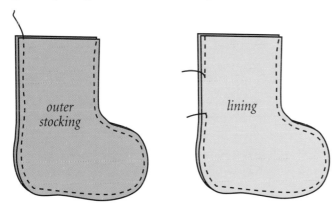

outer stocking

lining

❼ Turn the outer stocking right side out. Place it in the lining stocking with right sides together. Stitch the two together at the top.

❽ Turn through the opening in the lining and stitch the opening closed by hand or machine. Press

❾ Form a loop with some ribbon and stitch in place as a hanger.

lining

Poinsettia Towel

*C*hristmas is the time of year when everyone is busy, busy, busy! No matter how much there is to be done, we sewers always think of just one more thing to make for that special person who has been in our thoughts. This towel is a quick and easy project. We did ours on a fingertip towel, but it could easily have been done on anything from a sweater to a napkin, or even a Christmas ornament and been equally gorgeous.

Supplies

Fingertip towel
13mm silk ribbon: Spark Organdy in dark green and two shades of red
7mm silk ribbon: light yellow

❶ These stitches are all elongated lazy daisy stitches but have a unique appearance because of the wide width and sheerness of the Spark Organdy. Position the leaves according to the diagram, then add the dark red petal, then the light red petals.

❷ Finish the center with light yellow bullion stitches in a circular arrangement.

French knot 7mm

lazy daisy 13mm chiffon

Fabric Covered
Glass Ball Ornaments

Christmas is when the child in each person comes to the surface—the favorite time of year for shopping, parties, gift giving, and decorating! Whether your Christmas decorations are all synchronized with color and theme or a collection of ornaments and decorations that have accumulated through the years, they all add up to beautiful. Our tree holds many handmade ornaments received as gifts and made by our children as they were growing up. (I keep suggesting they take them home and add them to their trees, but somehow they always stay on our tree. Of course, there are the jokes and teasing over who did a better job. This dates back to when they were five and six!) I still have ornaments I received from students when I was teaching school, and that was many years ago.

These embroidered ornaments would be beautiful hanging on your tree or given as gifts. We did ours in traditional colors, but you could adapt them easily to fit your color scheme or the scheme of the person who is receiving them. They can be hung on the tree with a ribbon to hold them or a regular ornament hook. They dangle very delicately.

Supplies

4″ glass ball ornaments
4 pieces white cotton batiste (12″ x 7″ each)
Adhesive stabilizer
Sulky metallic thread: gold, red, green variegated
4mm silk ribbon: over-dyed Christmas color
7mm silk ribbon: over-dyed Christmas color
13mm silk ribbon: Spark Organdy dark red,
    over-dyed Christmas color, green
Metallic ribbon floss: gold
DMC metallic floss: gold

Poinsettia Ball

lazy daisy 13mm

French knot 7mm

❶ Lay the 12″ x 7″ piece of batiste on a hoop with adhesive stabilizer.

❷ Refer to the diagram and work the poinsettias with lazy daisy petals and French knot centers. In the one poinsettia we layered Spark Organdy and 7mm over-dyed Christmas colors for some of the leaves. Hold these ribbons together and treat them as one ribbon.

❸ Fold the lower edge to the wrong side about 1/4″. Zigzag over the gimp. (This forms the finished edge and provides a cord for tightly gathering the bottom.)

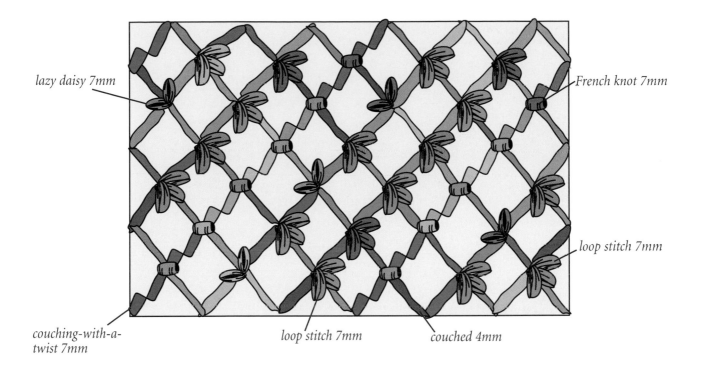

lazy daisy 7mm

French knot 7mm

loop stitch 7mm

couching-with-a-twist 7mm

loop stitch 7mm

couched 4mm

Diamond Square Ball

1 Draw a diagonal grid on a 12″ x 7″ piece of batiste with the lines approximately 1″ apart.

2 Anchor the end of the 4mm over-dyed Christmas ribbon. Stitch about 1″, carry the ribbon, and couch it in place until you reach the other side. Repeat across the grid.

3 Anchor the end of the 7mm over-dyed Christmas ribbon. Carry the ribbon to the first crossover of 4mm ribbon, work a French knot, then do couching-with-a-twist to the next crossover ribbon. Repeat the French knot. Repeat to the end of the fabric.

4 Use the same ribbon for the next row. Anchor the end. At the first crossover, work two lazy daisy stitches. At the crossover, work three loop stitches. Alternate these to the end of the row.

5 Use the same ribbon for the next row and at each intersection make three loop stitches.

6 Alternate these three rows until the second half of the grid is complete.

7 Fold the lower edge to the wrong side and zigzag over the gimp thread (any heavy thread or cord).

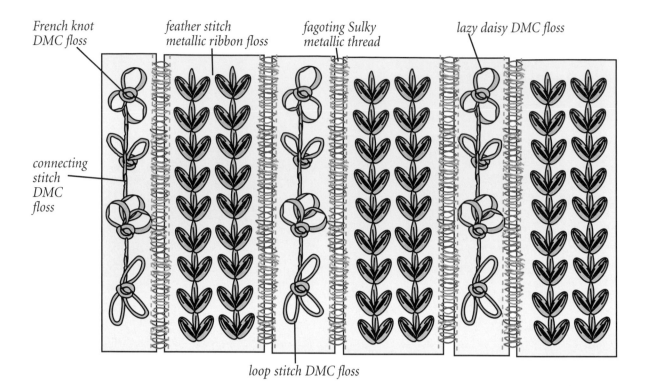

French knot
DMC floss

feather stitch
metallic ribbon floss

fagoting Sulky
metallic thread

lazy daisy DMC floss

connecting
stitch
DMC
floss

loop stitch DMC floss

Metallic Ball

❶ Cut a 12″ x 7″ piece of fabric into three strips 7″ x 1½″ and three strips 7″ x 2½″.

❷ Join these strips with fagoting, using Sulky metallic thread in the machine. See page 44 for fagoting directions.

❸ Work a stabilizing stitch with metallic thread also.

❹ With gold metallic ribbon floss, work two rows of feather stitches in the wider sections. We alternated our feather stitch rows.

❺ In unworked rows, work lazy daisy stitches with gold metallic DMC floss for leaves and loop flowers. Use the same floss for the French knot flowers. Couch the connecting stems.

❻ Fold the lower edge to the wrong side and zigzag over the gimp.

❼ When all the sections have been decorated, fagot the fabric ends together to make a cylinder. You will sew into the cylinder with the stabilizing stitches, but it's short enough to work easily.

Assemble the Balls

❶ Gather the lower edge by pulling the gimp cord tightly. When stitching the cylinder, be careful not to stitch over the gimp.

❷ After pulling tightly, knot to hold in place. Position the tassel or looped silk ribbon and stitch by hand to hold it in position. (If you're satisfied with the tightness of the gathering, you can leave the bottom undecorated.)

❸ Remove the hanger from the glass ball. Place the glass ball in the fabric, being careful to leave the open hole centered at the top.

❹ Push the extra fabric into the hole of the glass ornament, making small folds to evenly distribute excess fabric. (Tweezers work well.)

❺ Replace the hanger in the ball. Bend the metal cap outward if necessary. The clear glass ball inside the lightweight batiste will show light through them and almost glow as they dangle from your tree.

Battenburg Lace Ornaments

Supplies

2″-3″ Battenburg lace doilies

Adhesive stabilizer in hoop (You can place 3-4 doilies in the hoop, depending on the hoop size and size of doilies.)

4mm silk ribbon: dark green

7mm silk ribbon: over-dyed dark red, dark green, avocado, brown

Opalescent cord

DMC gold metallic floss

Poinsettia

❶ With 7mm avocado, work three large (1″-1¼″) long lazy daisy stitches for the poinsettia leaves. (By giving a twist to the 7mm ribbon you get the effect of a leaf.)

❷ Make five to seven long lazy daisy stitches to form the lower petals of the poinsettia with 7mm over-dyed dark red ribbon.

❸ Make four to five long loop stitches with 7mm red ribbon over the lazy daisy petals. (This gives the effect of a double poinsettia flower.)

❹ The center is made with DMC gold metallic floss worked in French knots. (These are the actual flowers on a poinsettia.)

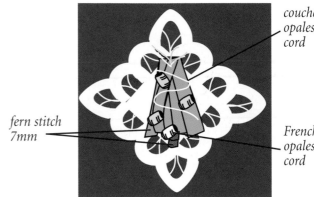

French knot metallic floss

lazy daisy 7mm

loop stitch 7mm

Tree

❶ Work the trunk with 7mm brown ribbon in a fern stitch. Start at the bottom, concealing the end and work so the top end will be covered with the green tree.

❷ Start at the bottom left of the tree and work a fern stitch with 7mm green ribbon. Be careful to conceal the end of the ribbon. Stitch to the top of the tree and anchor. Stitch to the bottom and repeat. When forming the tree, overlap the ribbon at the point of the tree and fan as you get to the bottom.

❸ The balls on the tree are made with French knots of DMC gold floss and opalescent cord.

❹ The garland is opalescent cord couched to the tree.

❺ The tree top is made with several small pieces of the two decorating cords tacked to the top. The ends are left to fray to give the "star" a sparkly appearance.

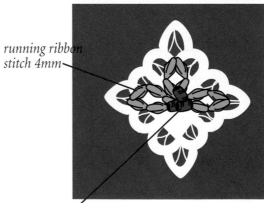

couched opalescent cord

fern stitch 7mm

French knot opalescent cord

Holly

❶ Start at center of the doily and work the running ribbon stitch in the shape of holly leaves. We made three leaves.

❷ With 7mm over-dyed red ribbon, work French knots (berries) to fill the center.

❸ Remove the extra stabilizer backing.

running ribbon stitch 4mm

French knot 7mm

Holiday Scarf & Barrette

*S*pruce up last year's outfit with an elegant new scarf and barrette! You'll sparkle all night long with the glistening beads and sparkly ribbons we've used.

If you can't find a barrette form, you can use foam core as a base. We used a smaller version of the scarf design, then placed it on the form and hand stitched it in place. Stitch the barrette on the back and off you go to the party!

Supplies

1½ yards rayon or silk with a black-on-black woven-in design
1 yard 6″ rayon silky fringe
Rectangular barrette cover kit (ours was 105mm x 45mm by Fibrecraft)
Black regular weight sewing thread
2 yards 25mm black sheer organza ribbon
1 yard 40mm black-on-black sheer striped organza ribbon
7mm ribbon: sheer organza black
4mm ribbon: black
2mm metallic cord: black
Metallic ribbon floss: gray/black
Black beads

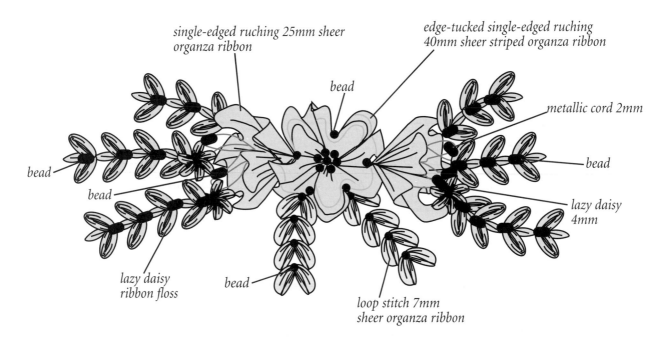

single-edged ruching 25mm sheer organza ribbon

edge-tucked single-edged ruching 40mm sheer striped organza ribbon

bead

metallic cord 2mm

bead

bead

bead

lazy daisy 4mm

lazy daisy ribbon floss

bead

loop stitch 7mm sheer organza ribbon

Holiday Scarf

❶ Cut two scarf pieces 16″ x 52″ from rayon or silk.

❷ Set one aside and embellish the other. Locate the center of the 16″ end of the scarf and mark it with a chalk marker, measuring up 6″ from the end. Start by sewing the center flower with 40mm sheer striped organza ribbon. Add beads to the center and on the edge tucks.

❸ Add the single-edge ruched flowers on either side, using 25mm sheer organza ribbon. String some beads on the metallic cord before attaching it to the center of the flowers.

❹ Add several lazy daisy flowers using 4mm ribbon with beaded centers.

❺ Add trailing vines under the center flower with loop stitched 7mm sheer organza ribbon and beaded centers.

❻ On each side, make branches with the feather stitch sewn with gray/black metallic ribbon floss. Add beads as you go along.

❼ Repeat the above embroidery on the other end of the scarf.

❽ Construct the finished scarf by placing it right sides together and stitching the long edges. Press.

❾ Turn in the raw edges on each end and press. Cut the fringe in half and place one piece on each end, pinning it in place. Stitch the fringe in place, sewing the ends shut at the same time.

Holiday Barrette

1 Stitch a smaller version of the scarf design onto a piece of rayon or silk large enough to cover the barrette form. Center the embroidered design on the form, turn the excess fabric to the back, and stitch in place.

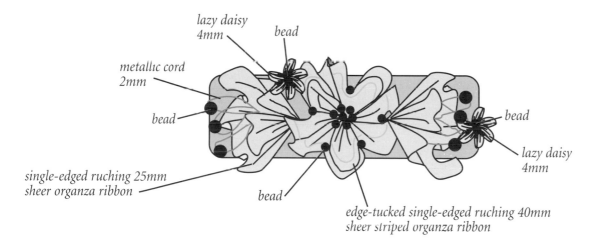

lazy daisy 4mm

bead

metallic cord 2mm

bead

single-edged ruching 25mm sheer organza ribbon

bead

bead

lazy daisy 4mm

edge-tucked single-edged ruching 40mm sheer striped organza ribbon

Silk Ribbon Embellished Latticework Vest

We were inspired by the vest on the September 1996 cover of Threads (#66) magazine. Lyla Messinger made the vest and wrote the article, giving several alternatives for constructing the latticework vest. We chose the method utilizing the bias binder foot. All the details follow to construct the vest. Make the vest first, then embellish with ribbon embroidery.

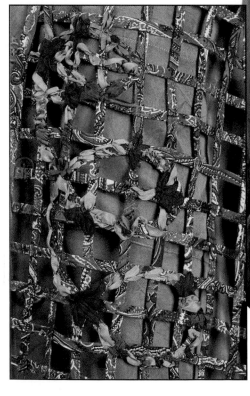

Supplies

Bias binder foot for your sewing machine
All purpose sewing thread to match the fabric
Simple vest pattern without darts
2 yards rayon challis print or solid
Rotary cutter and mat
Rotary cutting ruler

1 pkg. iron on stabilizer (such as Totally Stable by Sulky)
Teflon press sheet
7mm ribbon: dark red, olive green, plum
4mm ribbon: plum, olive, khaki, yellow/green, red, mauve

Make the Vest

1 Cut two vest backs from the challis fabric and set aside. Cut out the vest front from the stabilizer. Mark the seam lines and straight grain lines with a permanent marker. Following the grain line, use the rotary cutting ruler and mark grid lines 1″ to 1½″ apart. Measure the lines and add them up to get an idea of the total length of bias strips you need to sew. Add a bit extra to be safe.

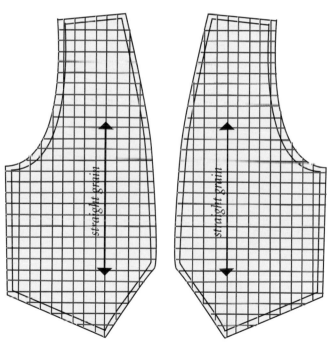

2 Fold the remaining fabric in half and then on the diagonal. Cut four bias strips 1½″ wide. Measure and be sure it's sufficient to bind the edges of the vest. Cut additional if needed and set aside to be used to bind the finished vest.

3 Cut the remaining fabric into generous 1″-wide bias strips.

4 Set the sewing machine for regular straight stitching and put on the bias binder foot. Cut the end of a 1″ strip into a point and thread it into the bias binder foot, using a straight pin to prod it along if necessary. Start stitching and check to be sure the stitching lies near the edge of the strip. Adjust the foot or the sewing machine's needle position if needed. Continue stitching the remainder of the strips. Because the pattern, grid size, and fabric width are all variable, you may have too many strips but you shouldn't run out.

5 Lay out the grid pattern with the "glue" side up. It's difficult to center the strip on a mark so line up the edges against the lines. On the right front, align them to the right of the line and on the left front, align them to the left of the line. Lay the vertical strips first, with the longest strips first, then weave over and under and complete the horizontal strips. When you are satisfied with the arrangement, place the Teflon press sheet on top and iron the strips in place.

6 Shape some of the leftover strips into free form curves as shown and steam them with the iron. Place them on the vest front and press in place.

7 Stitch all around the outer edge on the seam line and straight stitch or bartack the joints where the strips cross. Tack the free form curves in place the same way. Tear off the stabilizer.

8 To finish the vest, trim the seam allowance away from the areas shown by blue lines.

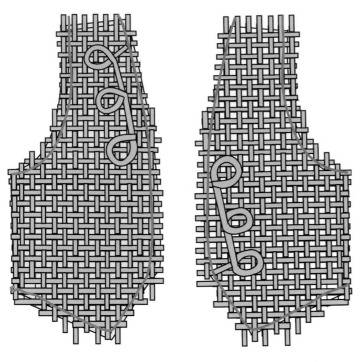

9 Apply the 1½″ binding strips around the front edge and bottom of the vest front and the sleeve opening. Join sufficient strips end to end and fold the long strip in half lengthwise and press.

10 Place the right side of the binding on the wrong side of the vest with the raw edges even. Stitch 1/4″ from the edge.

11 Bring the binding to the front and press. Topstitch in place.

12 Place one back piece right sides together with the two fronts and stitch the shoulder and side seams.

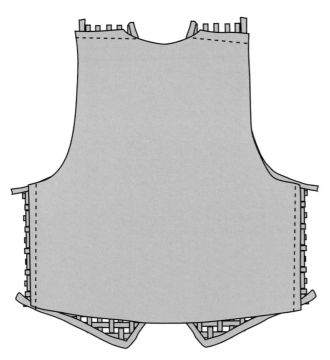

13 Leave the pieces in the same position and place the other vest back in position, right sides together, so the woven fronts are sandwiched between the two backs. Stitch in the following order: both shoulders; one side seam; other side seam, leaving a 4″ opening in the center; neck (be careful not to catch the woven fronts in this seam); two armholes (be careful not to catch the woven fronts in this seam).

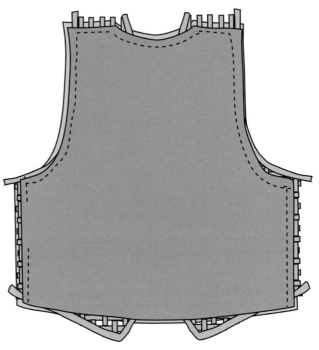

14 Turn the vest right sides out through the bottom. Check to be sure the woven front lies properly and didn't get caught in the neck or armhole seams. Press.

15 Pull the bottom inside out through the hole in the side seam and stitch. Turn and press.

16 Hand stitch the opening shut.

Ribbon Embroidery

❶ Follow the curved designs and make a series of silk ribbon flowers and leaves. Utilize the lattice that crosses within the curves as well. Follow the diagram and have fun!

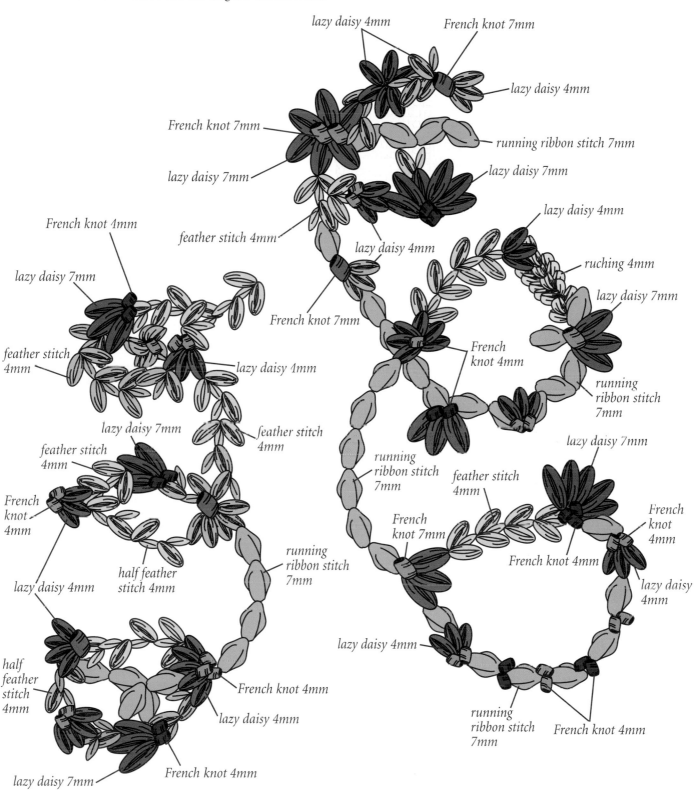

lazy daisy 4mm

French knot 7mm

lazy daisy 4mm

French knot 7mm

running ribbon stitch 7mm

lazy daisy 7mm

lazy daisy 7mm

lazy daisy 4mm

ruching 4mm

lazy daisy 7mm

French knot 4mm

lazy daisy 7mm

feather stitch 4mm

French knot 7mm

lazy daisy 4mm

feather stitch 4mm

lazy daisy 4mm

French knot 4mm

lazy daisy 1mm

running ribbon stitch 7mm

feather stitch 4mm

lazy daisy 7mm

feather stitch 4mm

running ribbon stitch 7mm

lazy daisy 7mm

French knot 4mm

feather stitch 4mm

French knot 4mm

French knot 4mm

lazy daisy 4mm

French knot 7mm

half feather stitch 4mm

running ribbon stitch 7mm

lazy daisy 4mm

half feather stitch 4mm

French knot 4mm

lazy daisy 4mm

lazy daisy 4mm

running ribbon stitch 7mm

French knot 4mm

lazy daisy 7mm

French knot 4mm

Photo Transfer Album Cover

January

Access to a color photo copy machine is necessary with the photo transfer paper. Any quick copy store will be able to perform the service for a nominal fee.

We transferred our photos to fabric first and took them with us when we chose the fabrics to get the right colors. Old faded photos like ours look better with soft muted pastels, whereas brightly colored photos would look great with brighter jewel tones.

Remember, you'll be adding ribbon embroidery, so stick to small prints, all-over flowers, or geometric designs on the fabric. A tone-on-tone, white-on-cream is nice too.

Supplies

Photo album approximately 9″ x 12″
1 yard 100% cotton muslin (do not pre-wash)
1 pkg. Quiltmakers Photo Transfer Paper™
1/2 yard fleece or lightweight cotton batting
Photos (photos will not be harmed)
1/8 yard each of three coordinated print fabrics
2mm ribbon: medium green

4mm ribbon: pale pink, medium pink, taupe, ivory, medium green, dark green
7mm ribbon: mauve pink, medium green, taupe or colors to coordinate with fabric
Regular weight sewing thread or hand quilting thread in both contrasting and matching color

Make the Fabric Cover

❶ Transfer your photos to the muslin following the manufacturer's directions. After you have them transferred, cut them apart, leaving a 1/4″ seam allowance.

❷ Prepare the fabric for the cover. Cut a piece 35″ x 16″. If your album is a different size, measure the height and width as shown. Then add 12″ to the width and 4″ to the height. We used a standard three ring binder (readily available at office supply stores) and then inserted photo pages.

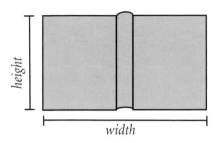

height

width

❸ Cut the fleece or batting the same size. Fold the cut fabric around the album, centering it, and use chalk or an air-soluble marker to indicate the front of the album where you'll place the photo patchwork.

❹ Cut one strip 2½″ wide x 45″ from each of the three coordinated print fabrics.

❺ Assemble the patchwork first then embellish it with ribbon embroidery. Begin by threading the machine with regular sewing weight thread to match the muslin. Use a zigzag stitch to stitch the fleece or batting to the wrong side of the muslin, stitching around the edges of the fabric. As you stitch the patchwork and ribbon embroidery through both layers, it gives a nice quilted effect.

❻ Switch to a regular straight stitch and randomly stitch the three strips cut from the coordinating prints to one side of each photo, with right sides together. Sew them clothesline style as shown, using a 1/4″ seam allowance.

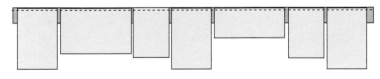

❼ Cut them apart and press the seam allowance to one side. Randomly choose a side without a strip and repeat as shown.

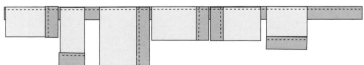

❽ Repeat until all the sides have strips of the print fabric sewn to them. Press any remaining seam allowances to one side.

❾ Lay them out in the area you marked as the front of the album. Fold the edges under and pin in place, rearranging them until you have a pleasing design. Depending on how many photos you transferred, you will probably have some left over. These can be used in a quick project such as an ornament .

❿ Thread the machine with contrasting sewing thread and stitch the edges down. We used the "mock hand quilting" stitch on our sewing machine. You can also stitch them by hand using a running stitch.

Ribbon Embroidery

❶ Refer to the diagram and stitch the ribbon embroidery. Start with 4mm taupe and do the chained knots.

❷ For the border shown at the bottom, mark dots about 5/8″ apart with an air-soluble marker. Use 4mm medium pink ribbon to make a lazy daisy stitch, pointing up on each of those dots, cutting the ribbon between each one. Use 2mm medium green ribbon and stitch two lazy daisy stitches at 45 degree angles at the base of the first medium pink lazy daisy. Make a French knot and stitch to the base of the next medium pink lazy daisy. Bring the ribbon and tack it in place. Continue across the row.

❸ Again, refer to the diagram and stitch the remaining embroidery.

Cover the Album

❶ To finish the album cover, fold under 1/4″ on each of the short ends and press. Place the cover around the album and pin. Be sure you close the album because the open measurement is smaller than the closed. Mark the fold line you pinned and take it off the album.

❷ Remove the pins and use the marks to fold it right sides together and stitch as shown.

❸ Trim away the excess fabric where you stitched and turn to the right side. Leave the remaining extra fabric to extend down about 2″ into book.

❹ Place the cover on the album. Cut a facing large enough to cover the uncovered center area plus 1″ extra all the way around. With the three ring binder, you should be able to slip the fabric under the metal ring portion. Otherwise, bring the fabric up to it. Hand stitch in place, turning the edges under or use fabric glue or a glue gun to hold as needed.

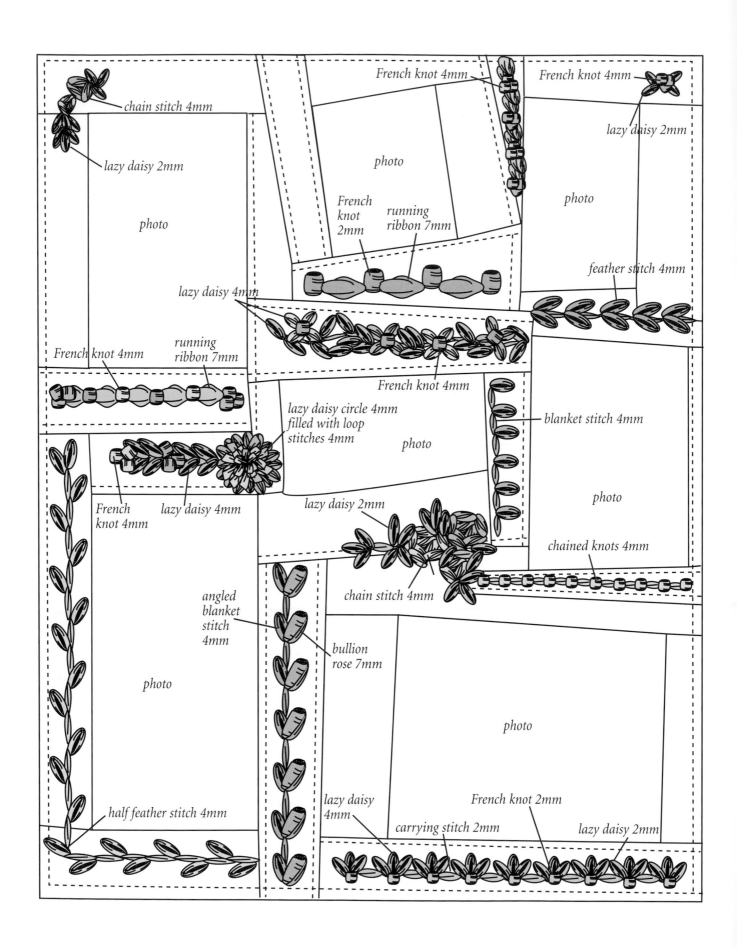

chain stitch 4mm

lazy daisy 2mm

photo

French knot 4mm

French knot 4mm

lazy daisy 2mm

photo

photo

French knot 2mm

running ribbon 7mm

feather stitch 4mm

lazy daisy 4mm

French knot 4mm

French knot 4mm

running ribbon 7mm

lazy daisy circle 4mm filled with loop stitches 4mm

blanket stitch 4mm

photo

photo

French knot 4mm

lazy daisy 4mm

lazy daisy 2mm

chained knots 4mm

chain stitch 4mm

angled blanket stitch 4mm

bullion rose 7mm

photo

photo

half feather stitch 4mm

lazy daisy 4mm

carrying stitch 2mm

French knot 2mm

lazy daisy 2mm

*P*hoto transfer is currently SO popular! It started its climb to the top with memory albums and memory quilts, but can be used virtually anywhere. We have made the perfect gift for almost any holiday for the proud parent, grandparent, or friend. The apron is quick and easy, but looks as if we slaved for hours. We chose ribbons to coordinate and contrast with the colors in the photo. You can repeat ours or choose your own to coordinate with the garment you are embellishing or to accent the photo.

Supplies

Apron (ours has Battenburg lace) or other clothing item
Photo transfer paper
Color photo (photo will not be harmed)
4mm silk ribbon: rust
7mm silk ribbon: over-dyed olive green, turquoise
13mm silk ribbon: lavender edge-dyed

❶ Transfer the photo to the apron, following the manufacturer's directions.

❷ Anchor the end of 7mm olive ribbon at the upper left side of the photo. Make a lazy daisy leaf then twist the ribbon and carry it approximately 1/2″.

❸ Leave the stem ribbon connected and work a lazy daisy flower using 4mm rust ribbon.

❹ Continue with a twisted stem stitch for another 1/4″, make three lazy daisy leaves, then continue the twisted stem stitch 1/4″.

❺ With 7mm turquoise ribbon make a loop stitched flower. Continue with olive to make a lazy daisy leaf and twisted ribbon stem for 1/2″.

❻ With 13mm edge-dyed lavender, work elongated bullion flowers. Finish these with loop stitched leaves. Continue with the stem for 1/2″ and add another bullion flower with the lavender ribbon.

❼ Add another loop leaf and more twisted stem.

❽ Add a rust French knot flower, a looped leaf with 7mm olive, and more twisted stem.

❾ Make loop stitches with 7mm turquoise ribbon and continue the twisted ribbon stem.

❿ A lazy daisy leaf is next and more twisted stem.

⓫ Next comes a ruched edge morning glory made with 13mm edge-dyed lavender ribbon and another 1/2″ of twisted stem, then three looped leaves.

⓬ Finish off the edging of the photo with three lazy daisy stitches made with 4mm rust ribbon.

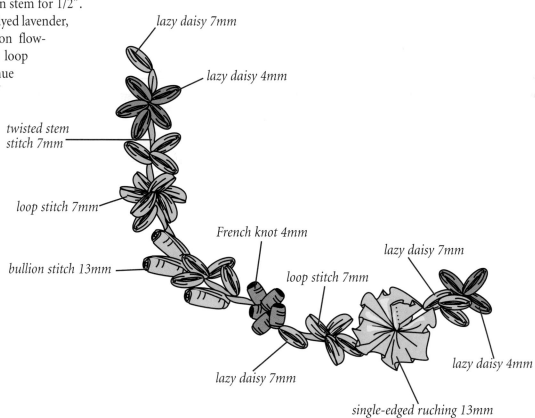

lazy daisy 7mm

lazy daisy 4mm

twisted stem stitch 7mm

loop stitch 7mm

bullion stitch 13mm

French knot 4mm

loop stitch 7mm

lazy daisy 7mm

lazy daisy 4mm

lazy daisy 7mm

single-edged ruching 13mm

Victorian Pillow

If any month signifies love and romance, it has to be February. Valentine's Day is the oldest holiday devoted to love and will never be overtaken by Sweetest Day or any of the other "newer" holidays. Valentine's Day makes us think of cupids, hearts and flowers, soft sentimental music, and just two of you.

Our Victorian Pillow helps spread the mood. It could be used in a dressing room, on a bed or chair, or simply to remind that special person that the holiday is near, lest you be forgotten!

Supplies

1/2 yard moiré faille taffeta

2 crochet heart shape lace doilies

14″ pillow form

4mm silk ribbon: medium pink, mauve, grayed green, olive green, light pink

7mm silk ribbon: green, grayed green, pink, over-dyed Christmas (shades from grayed pink, white, green), over-dyed pastel pinks, over-dyed shades of pink, over-dyed shades of red, light olive, shades of lavender

13mm silk ribbon: grayed lavender, edge-dyed green, edge-dyed shades of pink, edge-dyed shades of gray, Spark Organdy in light pink

Specialty threads: nubby greens, sparkly white, pink, gray

Beads: purple, pink/lavender, white, red

Upper Heart Ribbon Embroidery

1 Our heart doilies fit into a spring hoop. If yours don't, stitch them on the fabric before adding ribbon embroidery. Draw a heart shape on one doily with chalk or an air-soluble marker.

2 Start at the top and work French knots with 7mm lavender/pink over-dyed ribbon to form a point. Stitch a couple loop stitches with 7mm green edge-dyed ribbon to form the leaves.

3 Use 7mm over-dyed red ribbon in lazy daisy stitches to make the flower. The center has a couple small beads. Add more loop stitches with 7mm green edge-dyed ribbon to create the leaves on this side of the flower.

4 Make a dimensional flower with 13mm Spark Organdy. This is the single-edged ruching stitch. The ends in the center are stitched down and covered with beads. Do a fern stitched leaf in 7mm grayed green.

5 Loop stitches worked with two shades of 4mm pink form the next flower and lazy daisy stitches of 13mm edge-dyed green make the leaves.

6 Use 7mm over-dyed pink ribbon in the bullion stitch for the next flower. Make a few 4mm olive green leaves on the end of this.

7 The rose is made with 7mm over-dyed ribbon using the twisted ribbon stitch. Start with a triangle of stitches and keep working out. A running loop stitch brings you down and around the bottom point of the heart.

8 The next flower is 4mm pink in a lazy daisy stitch in a circle. Fill in the center with loop stitched nubby gray and pink yarn and finish with opalescent beads.

9 The next leaves are made with 4mm grayed green and a lazy daisy stitch. Immediately to the right of these leaves is another fern stitch made with a slightly darker shade of green 4mm ribbon.

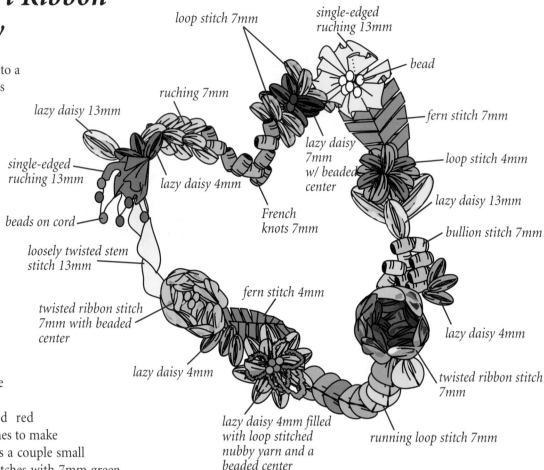

loop stitch 7mm

single-edged ruching 13mm

bead

fern stitch 7mm

ruching 7mm

lazy daisy 13mm

single-edged ruching 13mm

lazy daisy 4mm

lazy daisy 7mm w/ beaded center

loop stitch 4mm

lazy daisy 13mm

bullion stitch 7mm

French knots 7mm

beads on cord

loosely twisted stem stitch 13mm

twisted ribbon stitch 7mm with beaded center

fern stitch 4mm

lazy daisy 4mm

twisted ribbon stitch 7mm

lazy daisy 4mm

lazy daisy 4mm filled with loop stitched nubby yarn and a beaded center

running loop stitch 7mm

10 This flower is another twisted ribbon rose made with 7mm light pink edge-dyed ribbon. There are a couple lavender beads to finish the center.

11 Use 13mm edge-dyed light green and a loosely twisted stem stitch next. There's one lazy daisy stitch at the top of this stem.

12 The next flower is a fuchsia. Make three lazy daisy stitches in position with 4mm ribbon. Using 13mm ribbon, tack the squished end of the ribbon near the base of the lazy daisy stitches. Bring the ribbon around the needle and start ruching the edge of 13mm ribbon near the base of lazy daisy stitches and covering the end of the ribbon. You can add stamens in the center by stitching a cord strung with beads under the 13mm ribbon as you gather. Be certain to catch the ends of the cord under the ribbon as you make stitches.

13 Gather the ribbon over a 1/4″ area. When the fuchsia is full enough, work the end of the ribbon up and under to make a partial bottom row of gathering.

14 The last leaf in this heart is the double ruched leaf, tapering to a smaller size as it connects to the beginning of the heart.

Lower Heart Ribbon Embroidery

1 Draw a heart shape on the doily with chalk or an air-soluble marker.

2 Start at the upper left of the heart and make a loop stitched flower in 7mm pink. Below this flower are loop stitch leaves made with 4mm dark olive and an over-dyed green (1).

3 To the right of these leaves is a loop stitch flower made with nubby pink cord.

4 Back to the far left is a single-edge ruched flower using 13mm grayed lavender edged with fuzzy yarn. To make the edged ribbon, set the machine for regular sewing with the feed dogs up and a narrow zigzag stitch. Use monofilament thread in the top and bottom of the sewing machine. Stitch the fuzzy thread to the edge of the 13mm ribbon. We stitched a couple yards.

5 Use 13mm Spark Organdy ribbon for the next delicate flower, using the single-edged ruching stitch. Finish in the center with beaded nubby yarn (2).

6 To the right of this flower is a small loop stitch flower made using 4mm light pink ribbon and a sparkly cord. Add beads in the center.

7 Back to the far left of the heart make a small fern stitched leaf with 4mm dark avocado ribbon.

8 The next flower is lazy daisy stitches in 7mm Christmas colors over-dyed ribbon. Finish the center with a bullion knot in the same ribbon (3).

9 The next flower is made with 13mm gray edge-dyed ribbon and a twisted ribbon rose. Start in the center and do a couching-with-a-twist stitch in a concentric circle. Finish with a long green lazy daisy leaf.

10 Back at the far left is a 13mm Spark Organdy flower made with single-edge ruching. Finish the center of the flower with small red beads.

11 The next flower is made with 4mm medium pink loop

loop stitch nubby cord

loop stitch 4mm & sparkly cord with beaded center

loop stitch 7mm

twisted ribbon stitch 13mm

lazy daisy 7mm with beaded center

single-edged ruching 13mm

lazy daisy 7mm

loop stitch 13mm

fern stitch 4mm

single-edged ruching 13mm

running loop stitch 13mm topped with 7mm

beads

fern stitch 4mm

chain stitch 7mm

ruching 4mm

loop stitch nubby cord

loop stitch 7mm

calla lily stitch 13mm

lazy daisy & loop stitch 7mm

lazy daisy & loop stitch 7mm

chain stitch rose 7mm

Lower Heart

① loop stitch 4mm

② single-edged ruching 13mm with beaded center

③ lazy daisy with bullion center 7mm

④ loop stitch 4mm with bead center

⑤ lazy daisy 13mm

⑥ loop stitch 4mm

⑦ lazy daisy 7mm

⑧ loop stitch nubby cord with beaded center

⑨ lazy daisy 4mm with center of opalescent cord loop stitches and a white bead stitches in a circle and a white bead in the center (4).

⑫ That brings us to the rose. Go back to the far left and make the rose using the chain stitch worked in a circle with 7mm over-dyed red. Notice the natural shading of the over-dyed ribbons. Next are a couple lazy daisy leaves in 13mm edge-dyed green (5). Use 4mm forest green ribbon to make loop stitch leaves (6).

⑬ Under the chain stitch rose, make a loop stitch leaf with light green nubby cord. Make 7mm grayed green leaves with lazy daisy stitches (7).

⑭ Make the next loop stitch flower with nubby pink/gray shaded cord. Center this with small dark iridescent beads (8).

⑮ Start the next flower with a lazy daisy stitch done in 4mm light pink in a circle. Fill the center with loop stitches using opalescent cord and 4mm over-dyed light pink ribbon. Center this flower with a white bead (9).

⑯ Next is a half flower made using 7mm over-dyed pink ribbon and a lazy daisy stitch. Finish the center with three lavender beads. Make a leaf with 13mm edge-dyed light green ribbon in two large loop stitches and two small loop stitches.

⑰ Back to the far left for the last row. Use edged 13mm grayed lavender ribbon to form one calla lily stitch flower. (This assures the fuzzy edge staying out so it shows). Make leaves using 7mm green in a lazy daisy and loop stitch.

⑱ The next flower is a chain stitch rose using 7mm over-dyed lavender.

⑲ Make a lazy daisy and loop stitch with 7mm light avocado ribbon. Top this with one loop stitch rosebud made with 7mm pink over-dyed ribbon. A ruched 4mm forest green leaf is next. Make the fern with 4mm olive ribbon.

⑳ Make the last flower with 13mm Spark Organdy in light pink and 7mm over-dyed red ribbon layered one on top of the other. Then make a running loop stitch with the loops progressively getting smaller, tapering down to a point. That fills up our second heart!

Make the Piping

❶ To make the piping, you'll need five or six textured cords, silk ribbon, beads, a Spinster™, and a Seams Great™. Set your sewing machine to straight stitch for regular sewing

❷ Measure cords at least four times longer than the finished length.

❸ If using beads, string them on a fine smooth cord.

❹ Follow the directions on the Spinster and attach the ends of the cord with a slip knot. Hook one end on a doorknob, the other on the Spinster. Turn the Spinster handle until a twist is achieved.

❺ Double the cord and secure the end.

❻ Straight stitch over this cord, attaching it to the Seams Great.

Assemble the Pillow

❶ Arrange the hearts on the 15″ fabric sqaure. We put them at an angle, slightly overlapped. Stitch them on with invisible thread, about 1/2″ in, which gives the hearts a much freer look. (Isn't there a saying, "When you love someone, set them free?")

❷ Baste the piping to the pillow front. Cut two 11″ x 15″ pieces of moiré taffeta. Edge finish one 15″ side of each. Overlap these two finished sides to make a 15″ square. Baste together. Stitch back right sides to the front right side. Be certain that the stitching is close to the piping. Turn to the right side. Insert the pillow form and enjoy!

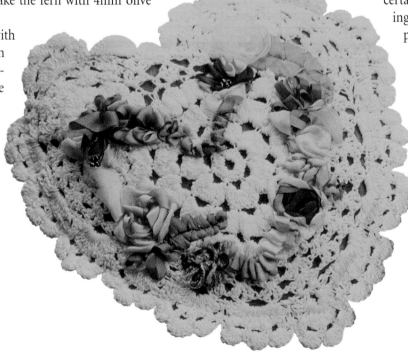

Quick Project
Valentine Cards

*F*ebruary's most popular day is without a doubt Valentine's Day—both for the young and the young at heart. It conjures up memories of the Valentine box at school and all those little cutout Valentines that were traded among the class. Of course, one got teased if a person of the opposite sex gave you a little bigger one or even taped a piece of candy or gum on it. We have taken to finding flat candy to enclose in Valentine cards to grandchildren faraway. (One way to keep them loving the Grandparents!)

We did some Quick Project Valentines—a good way to use scraps of fabric or ribbon.

Supplies

Blank note cards or paper (white and pink)
Battenburg shaped mini doilies
Scraps of dusty rose fabric (or fabric to match your color scheme)
Pieces of red ribbon (we used wire edged)
Sticky stabilizer
2mm silk ribbon: red
4mm silk ribbon: bright green, grayed green over-dyed, lavender over-dyed
7mm silk ribbon: pink, edge-dyed pink, red
7mm Spark Organdy: red, white
Beads, small white, purple, and opalescent; medium red and white

1 Do the ribbon embroidery on Battenburg lace shapes that have been laid on a sticky stabilizer to hold them in position in the hoop. Follow our illustrations or design your own. We attached our shapes to the paper cards with machine stitching, but you can also glue them on. Then pass them out to your favorite friends or that special Valentine!

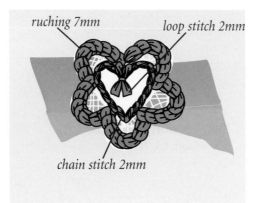

ruching 7mm

loop stitch 2mm

chain stitch 2mm

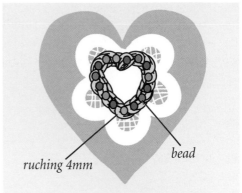

ruching 4mm

bead

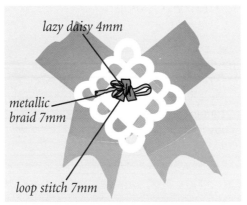

lazy daisy 4mm

metallic braid 7mm

loop stitch 7mm

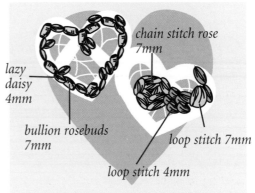

chain stitch rose 7mm

lazy daisy 4mm

bullion rosebuds 7mm

loop stitch 4mm

loop stitch 7mm

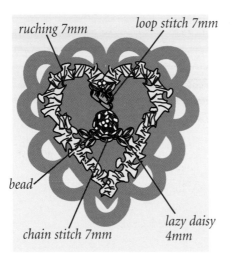

ruching 7mm

loop stitch 7mm

bead

chain stitch 7mm

lazy daisy 4mm

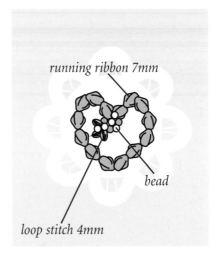

running ribbon 7mm

bead

loop stitch 4mm

Resources

Silk ribbons are becoming more readily available as their popularity grows. If the local fabric, craft, yarn, quilt, or sewing machine shop doesn't stock what you need, they may order it if you ask. Many supplies can also be purchased mail order. As you are looking for materials, ask for assistance and whether the store would special order for you. Don't leave a store without asking. Stores are always looking for product ideas and if we don't ask they don't know we want them.

YLI Corporation
161 West Main St.
Rock Hill, SC 29730
Customer Service (803) 985-3100
Orders (800) 296-8139

Nancy's Notions
333 Beichl Ave.
P.O. Box 683
Beaver Dam, WI 53916
Customer Service (920) 887-0391
E-mail nzieman@aol.com
Website http://www.nancysnotions.com

Clotilde, Inc.
B3000
Louisiana, MO 63353
Customer Service (800) 545-4002
Credit Card Orders (800) 772-2891

Quilters' Resource, Inc.
P.O. Box 148850
Chicago, IL 60614
Customer Service (800) 676-6543
Fax (800) 216-2374
Orders (800) 676-6543

Marie Duncan
E-mail andrewsewco@earthlink.net
Inquiries and questions

Bag Lady Press
P.O. Box 2409
Evergreen, CO 80437-2409
Purse findings
Customer Service (303) 670-2179
E-mail baglady@baglady.com
Website http://www.baglady.com
Orders (888) 222-4523

Ghee's
2620 Centenary Blvd. #2-250
Shreveport, LA 71104
Purse findings
Customer Service (318) 226-1701
Fax (318) 226-1781
E-mail ghees@softdisk.com
Orders (318) 226-1701

Lacis
3163 Adeline St.
Berkeley, CA 94705
Purse findings and ribbon
Customer Service (510) 843-7178
Fax (510) 843-5018
E-mail staff@lacis.com
Orders (510) 843-7178

Betty Farrell
E-mail JJFarrell2@aol.com
Inquiries and questions

L.J. Designs
76889 Barnsdale Road
Reno, NV 89511
Lattice vest pattern

Threads Magazine (#66, Sept. 1996)
The Taunton Press
P.O. Box 5506
Newtown, CT 06470
Lattice vest information
(203) 426-8171

The DMC Corporation
10 Port Kearny,
South Kearny, NJ 07032
Metallic floss or perle cotton

Index